A Child Born for Us

A
Child Born
for Us

The Infancy Gospel

David Neuhaus, SJ
with Terence Creamer and Debbie French

Paulist Press
New York / Mahwah, NJ

Library of Congress Cataloging-in-Publication Data available upon request.

ISBN 978-0-8091-5768-6 (paperback)
ISBN 978-0-8091-8934-2 (ebook)

Published by Paulist Press
997 Macarthur Boulevard
Mahwah, NJ 07430
www.paulistpress.com

Printed and bound in the
United States of America

Contents

Foreword vii
Cardinal Pierbattista Pizzaballa, Latin Patriarch of Jerusalem

Preface xi

About the Cover Icon...xv

Introduction 1

Chapter 1: Jesus's Ancestors 3

Chapter 2: Joseph, Son of Jacob.. 17

Chapter 3: Mary the Prophetess.. 29

Chapter 4: Nazareth and Bethlehem 43

Chapter 5: Jesus: A Child Is Born.. 59

Notes.. 75

Foreword

In his Regina Caeli address on the sixth Sunday of Easter in 2009, Pope Benedict XVI shared reflections on his voyage to the Holy Land. He said,

> The Holy Land has been called a "fifth Gospel" because in it we can see, indeed, tangibly feel the reality of the history that God brought about with men and women; beginning with the places of Abraham's life and including the places of Jesus' life, from the Incarnation to the empty tomb, the sign of his Resurrection. Yes, God entered this land, he acted with us in this world. But here we can say even more: the Holy Land, because of its history, may be considered a microcosm that sums up in itself God's arduous journey with humanity. It is a journey that implies together with sin also the Cross. Yet, with the abundance of divine love there is also always the joy of the Holy Spirit, the Resurrection that has already begun and is a journey through the valleys of our suffering towards the Kingdom of God. A Kingdom that is not of this world, but lives in this world and must penetrate it with his power of justice and peace.[1]

In referring to the Holy Land as the "fifth Gospel," Pope Benedict is citing the renowned expression of Saint Jerome, who made his home in a cave in Bethlehem, alongside the place of the nativity of Our Lord. There he avidly worked on the biblical texts, translating them and commenting on them. Jerome wrote, "Five gospels record the life of Jesus. Four you will find in books and the one you will find in the land they call Holy. Read the fifth gospel and the world of the four will open to you."[2]

The principal author of this book, Father David Neuhaus, SJ, has had the privilege of living in the Holy Land for most of his life. Over the decades, his love for the land and its people, as well as his faithful service in the Mother Church of Jerusalem, have been at the center of his identity and mission. For the past twenty-five years, he has been teaching Scripture in our diocesan seminary of the Latin Patriarchate of Jerusalem, not far from Bethlehem, and in many other institutions in Israel and Palestine. He has formed generations of seminarians, priests, men and women religious, and laypeople, endeavoring to awaken in them all the same love of Scripture that transpires from his teaching and writing. He has also worked in pastoral ministry with Arabic and Hebrew-speaking Catholics, with migrants and refugees, turning them all to the Word of God that animates our lives as Christians. Most importantly perhaps, he has taught catechism to children, composing a series of books for children, and so communicating fidelity to the Word to the future generations.

It was during some months that he spent in South Africa, the country of his birth, that Father David shared his love for the Scriptures in a series of Advent talks in the Jesuit Institute of South Africa. Terence Creamer and Debbie French set their mind to transcribing the lectures and convincing Father David to publish them. The dialogue between Father David, his collaborators, and those who actively participated in the talks provided a setting for an engagement with the infancy narratives in the Gospels. The fruit of the dialogue is this short collection of essays that takes us to Nazareth, Bethlehem, Jerusalem, and the other Holy Land locations that provide the backdrop for the entry of Jesus of Nazareth

Foreword

into our lives. *A Child Born for Us* offers the reader a penetrating and fascinating look at the texts that speak of Jesus's birth and infancy, focusing also on Our Lady, Saint Joseph, and the sacred history and geography of the Holy Land, all foundational to our identity and mission as Christians in our world today.

+ Cardinal Pierbattista Pizzaballa
Latin Patriarch of Jerusalem

Preface

This book is meant as a guide for the reader, individual, or group who would like a deeper understanding of the Gospel narratives of the infancy of Jesus. These narratives are complex texts that tell us more than one may think about who Jesus is and what relationship we are invited to have with him. The chapters in this book were originally conceived as an aid to living the Advent season more fully, preparing to receive the one who has been, who is, and who will be born for us—Jesus the Christ. However, the book is primarily about encountering the Incarnate Word through beautifully rich narratives that can deepen our faith at any point in the liturgical cycle.

The reflections in the book are linked to five themes, namely: Jesus's ancestors; Joseph, son of Jacob, father of Jesus; Mary the prophetess, mother of Jesus; the relationship between Nazareth, the town from which Jesus comes, and Bethlehem, the place of his birth; and, finally, Jesus himself and the moment of his birth.

This book engages in exegetical theology. Exegesis refers to the discipline of interpreting biblical texts through careful reading. Theology is the discipline of speaking about God. The conviction behind this book is that a careful reading of the biblical texts allows the reader to fully discover the relationship between God and the human person. Through understanding the plots, characters, and places described in the Bible, the reader can uncover the meaning of the Scriptures for their life, beyond simply explaining the literal or face-value meaning of the text.

Fundamental to this method of reading the New Testament is the conviction that it is written in shorthand. This means that the New Testament is written in the context of the Old Testament and that the reader must, thus, know the Old Testament—the Scriptures of Jesus, of the writers of the New Testament, and of the people of Israel. The Old Testament constitutes the longhand, with its use of language, its plots, characters, and places, essential to a full understanding and appreciation of the New Testament.

Reading backwards[1] from the New to the Old will be exercised throughout these pages in order to uncover depths of meaning that are revealed in the intertextuality between the New and the Old Testaments. The narratives of the Old and the New are truly connected through an intricate network of words, expressions, grammar, and syntax that reveals God's engagement with the reader, motivated by God's desire to bring the reader closer to other readers, constituting a community of sisters and brothers in communion with God.

Christians are not a "People of the Book" but followers of Jesus, the Incarnate Word. But the entire Bible is still an essential part of Christian life because it is the trace of Jesus, the One the Christian seeks. The texts in the Bible have been carefully composed, each word precisely chosen, and thus each expression evokes depths of meaning. Yes, these words were written hundreds of years ago for a very different audience, living in a very different culture, but those who truly take time to read, listen, and understand come to a marvelous realization: these texts are alive and real for readers of every generation, because at their core they are about relationship. They are about the reader's relationship with God, with others, and with creation, and about and God's relationship with humanity and creation. The Bible uses language that allows the reader to identify their needs, desires, and dreams in relationship with God, as well as God's desires and dreams for each of us. Through its captivating language, intriguing plots, complex characters, and evocative places, some of which will be encountered in this book, the texts reveal to the reader who they really are and how God comes to encounter them in the text.

The content is derived largely from a series of lectures delivered by Father David Neuhaus, SJ, in Advent 2023 for the Jesuit Institute in South Africa. The lectures are available on the Institute's YouTube page. Individuals and small groups may find these online lectures a useful complement to this book.

Each chapter is followed by suggested questions to facilitate further individual or group reflection.

USING THIS BOOK FOR GROUPS

The following is a guide for structuring group sessions. The framework is intended only as a suggested outline and can be used for in-person or online group sessions.

A good way to start a faith-sharing or spiritual group session is to play a spiritual song and then to quieten with a focused prayer. Lighting a candle also helps to create a quiet space, and is a visual reminder of the presence of God.

The prayer provided at the end of each chapter (or any other prayer, including a spontaneous prayer) can be used to open the session.

The group then reads the full text of the chapter aloud together, taking turns to read a few paragraphs each. If time does not allow for a full reading of the text, a group leader may preread the chapter and select specific parts of the text for group reading and reflection. In this case, group members may also preread the full text in preparation for the session, or may read the full text on their own after the session.

After reading the text aloud, group members read the full text or selected parts silently to themselves, making notes of any particularly meaningful points, new concepts, or insights. Individuals may also reflect on the questions listed at the end of each chapter in preparation for a group discussion. There are many questions listed, covering the key themes raised, but it is advisable to select only a few to stimulate reflection and discussion.

The group then reconvenes to discuss the questions and reflections based on the text.

The group session can be closed in prayer or with a spiritual song.

ACKNOWLEDGEMENTS

The authors would like to thank the entire team at the Jesuit Institute of South Africa for their support for the publication of this book. They express their gratitude to Cardinal Pierbattista Pizzaballa, Latin Patriarch of Jerusalem, for agreeing to write the foreword. They are also appreciative of all those who actively participated in the Advent series of lectures broadcast from the Jesuit Institute in December 2023. Their questions and comments have helped develop the themes presented in these pages. Finally, a word of thanks also to the team at Paulist Press who accepted the book for publication and edited it with sensitivity and expertise.

About the Cover Icon

The icon of the Nativity that features on the cover is a Byzantine-style icon. In it the old and the new intersect at the moment of God's Incarnation. The baby Jesus, wrapped in bands of cloth and laid in a manger, is at the icon's center, illuminating the dark tomb-like cave where the ox and the donkey also lie. Jesus enters a world where the people might have turned from God, but creatures still recognize God's wondrous work, evoking the Book of Isaiah when the prophet wrote, "The ox knows its owner, and the donkey its master's manger" (Isa 1:3).

A young Mary and older Joseph, who are kneeling, feature prominently, with Mary's hands prayerful and crossed over her heart and Joseph's open in praise. "She gave birth to her firstborn son and wrapped him in bands of cloth, and laid him in a manger, because there was no place for them in the inn" (Luke 2:7). Mary's prophetic act at the manger, a place meant for food, recalls the Last Supper, where Jesus says, "This is my body, which is given for you" (Luke 22:19). Her wrapping of the child also prepares us for Jesus's death and burial: "He took it down, wrapped it in a linen cloth, and laid it in a rock-hewn tomb where no one had ever been laid." (Luke 23:53).

The entire scene is illuminated by the star, which has guided the three men from the East to Jesus: "They shall bring gold and frankincense, and shall proclaim the praise of the Lord" (Isa 60:6). The rocky landscape is sparsely vegetated while a shepherd musician plays for the newborn child and the sheep gaze upon him, echoing: "Let the LORD, the God of the spirits of all flesh, appoint someone over the congregation who shall go out before them and come in before them, who shall lead them out and bring them in, so that the congregation of the Lord may not be like sheep without a shepherd" (Num 27:16–17).

The cave is flanked by angels, who also look on in wonder along with all the others in the scene. One of the angels is instructing a shepherd to come and see God being born as a human being. "Suddenly a great company of the heavenly host appeared with the angel, praising God and saying, 'Glory to God in the highest heaven, and on earth peace to those on whom his favor rests!'" (Luke 2:13–14).

Introduction

"But when the fullness of time had come, God sent his Son, *born of a woman, born under the law*, in order to redeem those who were under the law, so that we might receive adoption as children" (Gal 4:4–5). It is Saint Paul who gives the earliest reference to Jesus's birth. It is simply a fact that Jesus, like any other human person, was born of a woman. Paul, the earliest writer of texts included in the New Testament, wrote his Epistle to the Galatians in the mid–50s, about twenty-five years after Jesus's death on the cross. This single verse does not give a lot of information, but the information it does give is very important: that Jesus was indeed born like any human person, and obeyed the law like any Jew of his time. Jesus is truly a man and a Jew.

Neither Saint Mark, who composed the first book of the Gospel, perhaps in the early 70s, nor Saint John, who composed the last book of the Gospel contained in the New Testament, perhaps in the 90s, wrote anything about Jesus's birth or infancy. They both begin the Jesus narrative at the Jordan River, with the baptism. Therefore, in these reflections, the focus will principally be on the Gospel according to Saint Matthew and the Gospel according to Saint Luke, who each give slightly different accounts of Jesus's infancy.

Before looking closely at the two different versions, one might note the overwhelming similarities between the accounts of Matthew and Luke. Both Matthew and Luke underline that the conception of the child took place in miraculous circumstances. This was not just a simple human conception, but one in which God was directly involved. Both agree that Jesus was born in Bethlehem, the city of the great King David, although he would grow up in the family home in Nazareth. They both point to the fact that Jesus was descended from King David, not only a great king but also the ancestor of the long-awaited Messiah. They also concord on the identity of the child: he is the long-awaited Messiah of Israel and is also, in a very particular way, the Son of God. Matthew and Luke both say that he is the Savior and Redeemer. Both hint that, already from the time of his birth, some rejoiced in his coming and others rejected him. Furthermore, it is especially important to note that both writers rely heavily on the Old Testament, the Scriptures of the people of Israel, and that those Scriptures provide a language, a vocabulary, and a syntax to tell the Jesus story.

Many have asked what parts of these narratives are historical. Multiple volumes have been written on this very prickly issue. Certainly, Jesus was born as a child like any other person. However, the rest of the details in the text have been debated between those who argue that the story is probable or likely and those who say it is improbable and imaginative. Readers have been arguing for centuries about these issues, but what is important is to realize at the outset that neither Matthew nor Luke are historians in the modern sense. They are telling us who Jesus is for faith and what he means in the lives of those who believe in him. They are homing in on who he is in terms of his significance for all humanity, especially for the Church. Their purpose is not to relate a detailed factual history or to write a biography of the historical person, Jesus of Nazareth. Rather, they are both proclaiming Jesus as the awaited, anointed one ("Christ" in Greek and "Messiah" in Hebrew) and the Son of God.

Chapter 1

Jesus's Ancestors

The New Testament opens with a strange text: the genealogy of its central character, Jesus the Christ. Matthew, the writer of the book that is placed as the first of the twenty-seven books of the New Testament and the first of the four books of the Gospel, underlines in this carefully composed genealogy that Jesus is rooted in the history of the people of Israel, the people at the very center of the Old Testament. It is important to reread this text at the beginning of the discussion about "the child born for us."

> Book of the genesis of Jesus Christ, son of David, son of Abraham. Abraham begat Isaac, and Isaac begat Jacob, and Jacob begat Judah and his brothers, and Judah begat Perez and Zerah by Tamar, and Perez begat Hezron, and Hezron begat Aram, and Aram begat Aminadab, and Aminadab begat Nahshon, and Nahshon begat Salmon, and Salmon begat Boaz by Rahab, and Boaz begat Obed by Ruth, and Obed begat Jesse, and Jesse begat King David.
>
> And David begat Solomon by the one of Uriah, and Solomon begat Rehoboam, and Rehoboam begat

Abijah, and Abijah begat Asaph, and Asaph begat Jehoshaphat, and Jehoshaphat begat Joram, and Joram begat Uzziah, and Uzziah begat Jotham, and Jotham begat Ahaz, and Ahaz begat Hezekiah, and Hezekiah begat Manasseh, and Manasseh begat Amos, and Amos begat Josiah, and Josiah begat Jechoniah and his brothers, at the time of the deportation to Babylon.

And after the deportation to Babylon: Jechoniah begat Salathiel, and Salathiel begat Zerubbabel, and Zerubbabel begat Abiud, and Abiud begat Eliakim, and Eliakim begat Azor, and Azor begat Zadok, and Zadok begat Achim, and Achim begat Eliud, and Eliud begat Eleazar, and Eleazar begat Matthan, and Matthan begat Jacob, and Jacob begat Joseph the husband of Mary, of whom Jesus was born, who is called Christ.

So all the generations from Abraham to David are fourteen generations; and from David to the deportation to Babylon, fourteen generations; and from the deportation to Babylon to the Messiah, fourteen generations. (Matt 1:1–17)[1]

Undoubtedly the reader of these verses is overwhelmed by the strangeness of the names, many of them unfamiliar. This strangeness is an important element at the beginning of the narrative. The central character of the narrative is a man named Jesus, a first-century Jew from Galilee in Palestine. For him and those who wrote about him, all of whom were Jews, these names would be familiar. The long genealogy of this man roots him in the history of his people, the Jews. The reader should be warned that, in order to understand this collection of writings, known as the New Testament, it is important to have a knowledge of the Scriptures of the people of Jesus, which Christians call the Old Testament. Throughout the book written by Matthew, as well as those written by Mark, Luke, and John, and by Paul, James, Peter, and Jude, the reader is sent back to the Old Testament. It is only in the light of the Old Testament that the texts of the New can be fully comprehended. For the Christian, the New Testament in turn shines light on the Old Testament.

Matthew's careful composition, however, does not only list Jesus's ancestors; it does far more than that. By his constant demand to read backwards, from the New to the Old, Matthew is providing the reader with what the reader needs to grasp the turning point that is taking place with the entry of Jesus onto the scene of history. A close analysis of the expressions used in the composition of the genealogy is very revealing.

The genealogy begins with a carefully chosen expression drawn from the Old Testament: *book of the genesis*. Matthew, like all the other writers of New Testament texts, read the Scriptures in Greek, a series of ancient Jewish translations known as the Septuagint. Twice in the Book of Genesis there is reference to a "book of the genesis." "This is the book of the genesis of the heavens and the earth when they were created" (Gen 2:4). This phrase comes at the end of the description of the first creation account, which details God's acts of creation day by day. Using the same expression at the beginning of his book, Matthew hints at the fact that Jesus's coming into the world is a new creation. This new creation had been foreseen by Isaiah, who wrote, "For I am about to create new heavens and a new earth; the former things shall not be remembered or come to mind" (Isa 65:17). The same expression is also used at the beginning of the first genealogy of the descendants of Adam. "This is the book of the genesis of humanity on the day God made Adam, he made him in the likeness of God. Male and female he created them, and he blessed them and called them by their name Adam when he made them" (Gen 5:1–2). Matthew roots Jesus in the history of Israel, but Israel is rooted in the history of humanity, the descendants of Adam.

Old Testament Echo

Matthew's "book of genesis" is of a character named Jesus. For Greek readers of Matthew who knew the Scriptures of Israel, this man bore a very significant name. In Greek, the name *Jesus* (or *Iesous*) is the translation of the Hebrew name *Joshua* (or *Yehoshua*, sometimes shortened to *Yeshua*). Jesus in the New Testament evokes the Old Testament Jesus/Joshua, successor of Moses and main protagonist of the sixth book of the Old Testament. The first to draw attention to the Old Testament echo of Jesus's name, relating it to the figure of the Old Testament Jesus/Joshua, was Mark, who probably wrote before Matthew. In the sixth chapter of the Gospel of Mark, Jesus says to the disciples, "Come away to a wilderness place all by yourselves and rest a while" (Mark 6:31). The disciples have just returned from their first mission and Jesus proposes a Sabbath rest. However, the place he leads them to is a wilderness place, evoking the wilderness through which Moses led the people for forty years, a place where there is no food and no water. It is here that Jesus, in Mark's Gospel, will perform the first multiplication of loaves, revealing yet again who he is.

However, the link with the Old Testament figure of Joshua occurs as they arrive at this wilderness place, having crossed the Sea of Galilee. As they disembark, they discover that the crowds have preceded them. Jesus gets out of the boat, and Mark comments that when he sees the crowds, he sees that they are "like sheep without a shepherd" (Mark 6:34). This is a direct citation from Numbers 27, an important chapter in the wilderness narrative. Moses, knowing that he has come to the end of his life, intercedes for the people before God. In this intercession, Moses's greatness as a leader is apparent because he does not complain about his own fate of being unable to enter the land, but rather pleads for the people he has been leading for the past forty years, who will now be left without a leader. "Let the Lord, the God of the spirits of all flesh, appoint someone

6

over the congregation who shall go out before them and come in before them, who shall lead them out and bring them in, so that the congregation of the LORD may not be like sheep without a shepherd" (Num 27:16–17). God's response to Moses is that he should take Jesus/Joshua and establish him as his successor. "Take Joshua son of Nun, a man in whom is the spirit, and lay your hand upon him….You shall give him some of your authority, so that all the congregation of the Israelites may obey" (27:18–20). This scene takes place on the eastern banks of the Jordan River, from where the people can look beyond the river and see the land that they are about to enter.

Joshua will take over from Moses, who dies outside the land, and Joshua will lead the people into the land that God has promised them. The crossing of the Jordan will be a moment of baptism. The word *baptize* is explicitly used in the description of the crossing of the Jordan in chapter 3 of the Book of Joshua. "So, when those who bore the ark had come to the Jordan, and the feet of the priests bearing the ark were dipped [the word is *baptized* in both Hebrew and Greek] in the edge of the water" (Josh 3:15). As their feet are baptized, the waters part and the people cross on dry ground. Joshua can then begin his mission to make the land God's own land, given over to the people. His mission will involve casting out those evil nations who live in the land, a legion of evil spirits. In the New Testament, Mark begins his narrative of Jesus on the banks of the Jordan River at the moment of baptism. This is significant because it was there that Joshua, the son of Nun, was described as a man "in whom is the spirit" (Num 27:18). The figure of the first Jesus (Joshua)—a man in whom is the spirit, who takes over from Moses, who crosses through the waters of the Jordan in baptism and sets off to drive out the evil spirits in the land—prefigures the Jesus who is recognized as the Messiah.

Profound Connection

Matthew is certainly conscious of this profound connection between Jesus and Joshua, and he surely expects his reader to be as well. The naming of the child *Jesus* is a particular focus in the Gospel of Matthew. In the five episodes that follow the genealogy in chapters 1 and 2, Matthew underlines how the Scriptures of Israel are fulfilled in Jesus's coming into the world. In the first of the five, at the end of chapter 1 (1:18–25), Matthew describes the apparition of an angel to Joseph in a dream. In that initial dream, Joseph hears the words, "You are to name him Jesus, for he will save his people from their sins" (1:21). Focusing on the name Jesus, the angel explains the meaning of the name: "He will save his people from their sins." In Hebrew, the name is constructed from God's own name YHWH and is the word for salvation. This is expanded in the words of the angel, who refers to the act of saving the people from their sins.

Right from Matthew's first verse, at the beginning of the genealogy, Jesus is titled "Christ." The Greek word *Christ* is the translation of the Hebrew Messiah (*Mashiah*). All of the Gospel writers are convinced that Jesus is the Christ. The word Christ/Messiah is well known from the Scriptures of Israel and refers to those anointed by oil to serve in essential mediating roles between God and the people. Three particular roles in the Old Testament are styled christ/messiah (anointed ones). In Leviticus, the word is used for the first time in the Bible: "If it is the anointed priest who sins, thus bringing guilt on the people, he shall offer for the sin that he has committed a bull of the herd without blemish as a sin offering to the Lord" (Lev 4:3). The priest is described as anointed in his function of offering the sacrifice for sin.

However, this does not exhaust the use of the title *christ/messiah*. In the Historical Books, the anointed one is the king. For example, Samuel anoints David: "Then Samuel took the horn of oil and anointed him in the presence of his brothers; and the spirit of the LORD came mightily upon David from that day forward" (1 Sam 16:13). The anointing with oil is related here to the Spirit coming upon David. In a surprising text in the Book of Isaiah, a king from the nations is described as a christ/messiah: "Thus says the LORD to his anointed [christ/messiah], to Cyrus, whose right hand I have grasped to subdue nations before him and strip kings of their robes, to open doors before him—and the gates shall not be closed" (Isa 45:1). Significantly, this is the only use of the word *christ/messiah* in the Book of Isaiah.

There is a third function that is described as being anointed, namely the prophet. Whereas priests and kings are anointed with oil, the prophet is anointed with the spirit. One seminal text that refers to a prophetic anointing is the one Jesus reads in the synagogue of Nazareth at the beginning of his ministry according to the Gospel of Luke. "The spirit of the Lord GOD is upon me, because the LORD has anointed me; he has sent me to bring good news to the oppressed, to bind up the brokenhearted, to proclaim liberty to the captives, and release to the prisoners" (Isa 61:1). It is only in the Book of Daniel, composed at a much later period, that the word *christ/messiah* refers to an end-of-times savior figure. "Know therefore and understand: from the time that the word went out to restore and rebuild Jerusalem until the time of an anointed prince, there shall be seven weeks" (Dan 9:25).

Reading Backwards

The practice of reading backwards is necessary to continue with Matthew's text. Jesus Christ is described as the "son of David." It is important to identify that Jesus is not genealogically the son of David: rather, this too is a title. In 2 Samuel, God sends a message to David about a son that he will have who will reign forever. David's own son, Solomon, is not that son, as he ends his reign in dishonor and is buried. "When your days are fulfilled and you lie down with your ancestors, I will raise up your offspring after you, who shall come forth from your body, and I will establish his kingdom. He shall build a house for my name, and I will establish the throne of his kingdom forever. I will be a father to him, and he shall be a son to me" (2 Sam 7:12–14). David's son will be God's own son.

Likewise, when Matthew refers to "son of Abraham," the expression needs to be understood against the backdrop of the Scriptures of Israel. In the Book of Isaiah, Israel is referred to as the offspring of Abraham.

> But you, Israel, my servant, Jacob, whom I have chosen, the offspring of Abraham, my friend; you whom I took from the ends of the earth, and called from its farthest corners, saying to you, "You are my servant, I have chosen you and not cast you off"; do not fear, for I am with you, do not be afraid, for I am your God; I will strengthen you, I will help you, I will uphold you with my victorious right hand." (Isa 41:8–10)

Jesus comes as a fulfillment of all that Israel was called to be.

The first verse of Matthew's Gospel is amplified by the constant referring back to the Scriptures of Israel. This same method must now be applied to the actual genealogy. The genealogy recounts a long series of fathers begetting sons, a common literary genre in the Old Testament. Genealogies are found in different parts of Israel's Scriptures, most importantly in Genesis and in the first nine chapters of 1 Chronicles, a history rewritten in the light of the return to Jerusalem after the exile in Babylon. However, what catches the eye of the reader in this genealogy of Matthew are the times that the genealogical unit—a father begets a son—is appended by additional information.

The first time that the unit is appended with additional information is in verse 2: "Jacob begat Judah and his brothers."

10

Although many of the fathers mentioned would have had more than one son, brothers are only mentioned twice. The other time is "Josiah the father of Jechoniah and his brothers" (1:11). The significance of these two references to brothers might be the fact that the generation of Judah and the generation of Jechoniah both experienced a dramatic departure from the land of Israel: the first at the time of the descent into Egypt and the second at the time of the descent into Babylon. In Matthew's narrative, Jesus will also leave the land and descend into Egypt in chapter 2.

Another appendage to the simple genealogical unit takes place when, in five instances, mothers are introduced. The five women mentioned in the genealogy are Tamar, Rahab, Ruth, the woman called "the one of Uriah," and Mary. All five are surprising women. The first four evoke difficult episodes that might provoke scandal. Tamar played the prostitute to seduce her father-in-law, in order to get him to do justice by her (Gen 38). Rahab was a prostitute, and yet her faith in the God of Israel led her to save the two spies Joshua had sent into Jericho (Josh 2). Ruth was a Moabite, belonging to a people about which the law had said, "No Ammonite or Moabite shall be admitted to the assembly of the LORD. Even to the tenth generation, none of their descendants shall be admitted to the assembly of the LORD" (Deut 23:3). However, Ruth, through her faith, becomes a new Abraham, leaving her home, her land, and her gods to join the people of Israel in Bethlehem (Ruth 1:16–19). Bathsheba is not named but rather referred to as "the one of Uriah," underlining the shameful behavior of the man who committed adultery with her and then murdered her husband (2 Sam 11).

Furthermore, the first four women seem to be women from outside the people of Israel, representing the nations. This is certain for Rahab and Ruth, who are presented in the genealogy as being mother-in-law and daughter-in-law, a detail mentioned nowhere else in Scripture. Rahab was a Canaanite, belonging to a people that would be destroyed in the conquest of the land.

However, her faith brings her (and all in her household) salvation. Ruth was a Moabite, but her faith not only brings her inclusion into the people but leads her to become the great-grandmother of King David.

The fifth woman is Mary. She too is a surprise at the end of the genealogy, and her presence disrupts the simple genealogical unit of a father begetting a son. "Jacob begat Joseph the husband of Mary, of whom Jesus was born, who is called the Messiah" (1:16). The seeming scandal of Mary's pregnancy will lead the reader into the narrative of Jesus's coming into the world.

A further appendix is to be found in verse 6: "King David." Although David is the first king in the list, he is certainly not the last. However, none of the others bear the title king. The word *king* read back into the Scriptures of Israel provides an essential backdrop to the history of Israel. As a people, Israel was born emerging from slavery in Egypt through blood (on the doorposts of their homes on Passover night) and water (crossing the Sea and escaping Pharaoh's armies). When these armies have drowned, Moses stands on the shore and sings his song of victory. The last verse of this song is Israel's motto, "The LORD is king forever and ever" (Exod 15:18). Israel is called to be different from other nations in that they have kings of flesh and blood, but Israel's king is Israel's God. However, when Israel enters the land, the people seek to be like all other peoples, and hanker for a king. Almost always, the king is a profound disappointment, leading the people into sin. In Matthew's genealogy, David is titled *king* in a verse that points to one of his greatest sins, his adultery with Bathsheba and his murder of Uriah, her husband and his faithful soldier.

The evocation of the struggle over kingship in Israel will play out in Jesus's life too. When he was born, King Herod ruled. Herod learns from the three men coming from the East that "the child who has been born king of the Jews" (2:2) has come. He is revealed to be an unscrupulous "pharaoh" in his determination to kill the child who threatens his throne and, in the process, murders the babies in Bethlehem just as Pharaoh had done to the babies in Egypt at the time of Moses.

It is striking that in Matthew's genealogy, the great events in the life of the people are evoked only in their relationship with the characters who are named. However, there is one exception. One event is mentioned not once but twice. "Josiah begat Jechoniah and his brothers, at the time of the deportation to Babylon. And after the deportation to Babylon: Jechoniah begat Salathiel" (1:11–12). Clearly the deportation to Babylon had great significance for Matthew. What does this event represent in the Scriptures of Israel? The Babylonians conquered the Kingdom of Judah in 597 BCE and led the ruling elites into exile. After a failed rebellion, they then destroyed Jerusalem and its temple in 587 BCE. The total destruction of the kingdom, the cult, and the land were the death of the people. Josiah, a righteous king, had been followed by a series of sinful sons who led the people to destruction. God's great plans for the people were ruined and the people were buried in the tomb of an exile far from their land. Matthew would certainly expect the reader to stop reading in mournful silence after verse 11. The silence that should punctuate the reading is like the silence of a Holy Saturday for the people of God, called also the firstborn son of God (cf. Exod 4:22), which has died and is buried.

However, the genealogy continues. Among all the surprises in the genealogy, none is greater than the word *after*: "And after the deportation to Babylon: Jechoniah was the father of Salathiel" (1:12). What does *after* mean in the context of death and burial? God does not allow death and burial to be the last word. God will be faithful to God's promise and will not allow death to be victorious. Indeed, the central event in the life of the people of Israel in the Old Testament is the return from exile, the rehabilitation of Jerusalem and the reconstruction of the temple. These events are lived as a resurrection from the dead. In the Book of Isaiah, this is the good news.

How beautiful upon the mountains
   are the feet of the messenger who announces peace,
who brings good news,
   who announces salvation,
   who says to Zion, "Your God is king." (Isa 52:7)

The genealogy prepares the reader to enter the narrative about Jesus, who comes as king, victorious over death. Matthew will present Jesus as God's presence in the midst of God's people. This people is rooted in the Israel of the Old Testament and its language, vocabulary, syntax, and grammar form the language of Matthew and all the other writers of the New Testament. Reading backwards is an essential discipline to uncover the depths of meaning of the New Testament. At the center of Matthew's Gospel, at the end of the third of Jesus's five great discourses, the discourse on parables, Jesus says, "Therefore every scribe who has been trained for the kingdom of heaven is like the master of a household who brings out of his treasure what is new and what is old" (13:52). The reader is called to be just such a scribe.

The New Adam

Matthew's genealogy of Jesus is not the only one in the New Testament. Luke provides a very different one (Luke 3:23–38). Many readers have been troubled by the differences in these two genealogies and many interpreters have tried to resolve the differences.

Rather than harmonize the two very different texts, the reader is encouraged to notice the distinct contexts in which each genealogy is inserted. Matthew's genealogy, which progresses from Abraham to Jesus, is inserted where one would expect a genealogy to be—at the beginning. It introduces Jesus as rooted in the people of Israel.

Luke's genealogy, however, is inserted at a very different point in Luke's narrative. It is situated between the baptism of Jesus in the

Jordan and the temptation of Jesus in the wilderness. Reading backwards is no less important for Luke than it is for Matthew, for he too draws extensively on the Scriptures of Israel. However, his genealogy stretches from Jesus all the way back to Adam, son of God, at the very point at which Jesus is to show that he is the new Adam.

In the baptism, Jesus hears the heavenly voice say, "You are my Son, the Beloved; with you I am well pleased" (Luke 3:22). The reader, familiar with the Scriptures of Israel, is fully aware that this is not the first time that the Father has attempted to be father to a son. Adam, the first human, was created in God's image and likeness, like a son to a father. At the end of the Lukan genealogy, Luke will explicitly call Adam "son of God" (3:38). When Adam fails, God does not give up, ever faithful to the divine plan, and tries again with Israel, the people God called "my firstborn son" (Exod 4:22). Although more successful than Adam, Israel is too often unfaithful and chooses death over life. God is now trying again with Jesus. After the baptism, the reader familiar with the Scriptures of Israel must wonder, will it work this time? The genealogy follows the baptism and precedes the temptation to drive home the point: Jesus is a new Adam, who, unlike the first Adam, will remain faithful to the Father. In Jesus, humanity is renewed, and creation can be restored. As Saint Paul wrote, "For as all die in Adam, so all will be made alive in Christ" (1 Cor 15:22).

Group Discussion

Refer to the introduction for tips on conducting a group discussion.

Questions for further reflection (select a few questions from the list below that you feel will help stimulate reflection and discussion; you could also use your own questions):

1. Do you see any value in reading the New Testament "backwards from the beginning"—that is, allowing the Old to shine light on the New and the New to shine light on the Old?

2. How does your history and the history of your ancestors shine a light on your current life—both physical and spiritual?
3. What can you learn from your own history that could help you on your spiritual journey?
4. What comes to your mind when you read Matthew's genealogy backwards?
5. How do you respond to the link drawn between Jesus in the New Testament and Joshua in the Old Testament?
6. Does Jesus's baptism in the Jordan take on any added meaning when you consider the role of Joshua in the baptism of the people of Israel in the Jordan?
7. Do you have any reflections on Jesus as the new Adam, faithful to the father?

Chapter 2

Joseph, Son of Jacob

Joseph, son of Jacob, or Saint Joseph, as he is known in Christian tradition, is the central personality in the first two chapters of the Gospel of Matthew, which are also the first two chapters of the New Testament. They constitute the only narrative in the New Testament that focuses on Joseph.

The two chapters in question form a well-structured literary composition. The long genealogy at the beginning of the book (Matt 1:1–17) introduces Jesus by situating him in the generations that stretch from Abraham, the father of the faithful, to Joseph, the father of Jesus. The seventeen verses at the beginning of the New Testament are right at the place where the New Testament is joined to the Old in the Christian Bible. It is at this place that the reader is introduced to the figure of Joseph, son of Jacob, father of Jesus. Matthew underlines the planned nature of the development of history by concluding the genealogy with a symmetrical division. "So all the generations from Abraham to David are fourteen generations; and from David to the deportation to Babylon, fourteen generations; and from the deportation to Babylon to the Messiah, fourteen generations" (Matt 1:17). This neat presentation adds to the anticipation regarding what follows.

Following the genealogy, five episodes take the reader into Matthew's narrative. All five are embroidered around verses from the Scriptures of Israel (the Old Testament). These citations underline that the time of fulfillment has come. Four of these episodes focus on the figure of Joseph, presenting him as the ideal person of faith, the one who listens carefully to God's word and thus becomes the father, custodian, and protector of the child who is born. The five episodes are:

- the Annunciation to Joseph, embroidered around Isaiah 7:14: "Look, the virgin shall conceive and bear a son, and they shall name him Emmanuel" (Matt 1:23);
- the Magi following the star to Jerusalem, embroidered around Micah 5:2: "And you, Bethlehem, in the land of Judah, are by no means least among the rulers of Judah; for from you shall come a ruler who is to shepherd my people Israel" (Matt 2:6);
- Joseph's flight with the mother and child to Egypt, embroidered around Hosea 11:1: "Out of Egypt I have called my son" (Matt 2:15);
- the massacre of the babies in Bethlehem, embroidered around Jeremiah 31:15: "A voice was heard in Ramah, wailing and loud lamentation, Rachel weeping for her children; she refused to be consoled, because they are no more" (Matt 2:18);
- Joseph's settling in Nazareth, embroidered around an unidentifiable verse from Scripture: "He will be called a Nazorean" (Matt 2:23).

In the Gospel of Matthew, Joseph, son of Jacob, is presented, first and foremost, as a righteous man: "Joseph, being a righteous man" (1:19). That term, *righteous*, or *just*, refers to a man who lives fully according to the Law of Moses, known as the Torah. He is an

18

exemplary Jew. His righteousness is what identifies him in the narrative, preparing the reader for what follows, as Joseph is attentive to the word of God. Joseph is the son of Jacob, identified thus at the end of the genealogy, where it is written: "Jacob begat Joseph, the husband of Mary, of whom Jesus was born, who is called the Messiah" (1:16). Jesus here is called Messiah, as he is in the first verse of the Gospel, the one people are waiting for, the anointed one, the promised one.

The New Testament is written in shorthand, and in order to fully understand it the reader must know well the language, the vocabulary, and the ideas of the Old Testament. The New Testament is rooted in the Old. Hearing the New in the light of the Old gives it its fullest meaning. The New not only throws light on the Old; the Old also throws light on the New. Recognizing this, the reader should immediately identify the fact that Joseph, son of Jacob, is not the first Joseph, son of Jacob, encountered in the biblical narrative. In the first book of the Bible, there is another Joseph, son of Jacob, who is a luminary in the Old Testament. In the Gospel of Matthew, the father of the Old Testament Joseph, the Old Testament Jacob, appears early on in the genealogy. However, having had twelve sons, the son mentioned in the genealogy is not Joseph his eleventh son, but rather Judah, through whom the New Testament Joseph is descended.

It is fascinating to compare the two Josephs. These two characters, identified initially by the fact that they have the same name, have more in common than that, and the parallel between them allows the reader to get to know the New Testament Joseph in more depth. Getting to know Joseph in the New Testament depends to a large extent on rereading the chapters in the Book of Genesis where the first Joseph's story is told. The Old Testament Joseph, son of Jacob, is named for the first time in chapter 30 of Genesis. There it describes Rachel's naming him Joseph: "May the Lord add to me another son" (Gen 30:24). Rachel was the beloved but not the only wife of Jacob. She would give birth to two sons, both of them dearly beloved by their father. The Hebrew name *Joseph*, derived from the word "to add to," indicates that she is already praying for the birth of her younger son Benjamin. The name points to a certain lack of completeness; something else needs to come to complete this righteous man called Joseph. In the New Testament, that necessary addition will be the child that will be born to Mary; the child that is Joseph's son.

The parallels between Joseph and Joseph become even more revealing when the reader realizes that Joseph in the New Testament must be read through the prism of the first Joseph. It is essential to recall that Joseph is the last character who appears in Genesis, revealing an essential element in the relationship between God and the human person. After passing through the trials and tribulations of being sold into slavery by his jealous brothers and being accused falsely and imprisoned in Egypt, Joseph becomes a viceroy with the power to save his brothers, the very ones who had plotted to kill him. Even after he has forgiven them, they still have their doubts about whether they are indeed forgiven, and at that point, at the end of Genesis, Joseph reveals a principle that underlies the entire history of salvation: "Even though you intended to do harm to me, God intended it for good" (Gen 50:20). Indeed, humans do evil, but God is working hard to transform all that evil into good, a theme that is important in the New Testament too.

Righteous Men

The two Josephs are both righteous men who are seen to be compromised by women. The Old Testament Joseph, who had been sold into slavery in Egypt, has a problem with the wife of his master. Potiphar's wife lusts after Joseph and says to him, "Lie with me" (Gen 39:7). However, Joseph is a righteous man. Not only will he not commit that kind of impurity, but he will also not betray his master, even though he will pay a heavy price for his principles and spend time in prison. Matthew presents the New Testament Joseph as engaged to a woman named Mary who is found to be pregnant. This would have been a very troubling situation, as her husband-to-be would expect her to be a virgin. And if she is with child, that must imply that she is neither a virgin nor a virtuous woman. Although the reader knows that the child is from the Holy Spirit, Joseph does not know this when the narrative begins.

This dilemma gives the reader occasion to discover the righteousness of Joseph, her husband. He, "being a righteous man and unwilling to expose her to public disgrace, planned to dismiss her quietly" (Matt 1:19). This description reveals that Joseph is more than righteous. A righteous man would have the right to denounce the woman he is engaged to if she is pregnant, and her fate would probably be horrible. Who would believe that the Holy Spirit has impregnated her? Supposing she had been with another man and that she has become pregnant, she would be put to death. Yet Joseph, unwilling to expose her to the public disgrace of a trial or worse, decides to dismiss her quietly. This "trouble with a woman" will reveal Joseph as not only a righteous man, but also a merciful man, one who is in the image and likeness of God, who is both just and merciful. This interesting parallel between the two Josephs shows how the Old Testament shines light on the New.

Men of Dreams

Furthermore, the Joseph in the Old Testament is a man of dreams, dreams that lead him on a wild adventure—a salvific adventure. People in traditional cultures are aware that God speaks in many different ways. The unconscious that is expressed in dreams is a way in which God can communicate. When humans are fully conscious, they try to be in full control, and dreams are a way that God can break through. In modern times, Sigmund Freud, the founder of psychoanalysis, certainly gave great importance to dreams, as others dealing with the human psyche have similarly done. Early on, the Old Testament Joseph's dreams led him to lord it over his brothers, and they hated him for it. They sold him into slavery, but when he was in prison, he had dreams that saved the life of some and condemned others, and that would eventually lead him into the court of Pharaoh, where he read Pharaoh's dreams. These dreams would lead him to a role of great power, becoming a savior of those same brothers who had betrayed him. For when there was a famine, Joseph's interpretation of dreams enabled Pharaoh to store corn that would save the Egyptians as well as Joseph's own brothers who came begging for food.

The Joseph the reader gets to know in the New Testament is, likewise, a man of dreams. One of the great things about the New Testament Joseph was the recognition that, by listening closely to the word revealed in a dream and acting according to it, he was fulfilling his vocation to be Jesus's father. Jesus the child is under constant threat, and Joseph will preserve him through dreams. These dreams show his openness to listening carefully to words that lead him on an adventure, words that come from on high. The words are essential to his role in fathering Jesus, directing him to take care of the child and to keep him safe—traditionally a father's role. These dreams fill the narrative of Joseph in Matthew's composition. Four times Joseph dreamed that an angel of the Lord appeared to him. In Matthew 1:20, addressing the embarrassing situation of the pregnancy of Mary, the angel tells Joseph not to fear, to take Mary into his home, for the child within her is from the Holy Spirit. And so he does. Three more dreams in chapter 2 show how essential Joseph is to the story and that, without Joseph and his openness to the word in his dreams, there would be no Jesus. In fact, Mary would already have been stoned if Joseph had not been both righteous and merciful.

In a dream after Jesus's birth, an angel of the Lord appeared to Joseph and ordered him to take the child and go to Egypt (2:13), for indeed Herod, a wicked "pharaoh," rules in Jerusalem. This evil king, like the one at the time of the people's slavery in Egypt, is going to kill babies in order to try to wipe out the promised Savior, the one he perceives as competing with him to be king. Joseph's dream directs him to save the child, father the child, nurture the child, and protect the child. Later, if Joseph had not been focused, shutting his ears to the word, he would not have been open to another dream in Egypt, where an angel of the Lord appeared and said: "Arise, and take the young child and his mother, and go into the land of Israel: for they are dead which sought the young child's life" (Matt 2:20). Joseph's openness to his dreams plays an essential role, showing Joseph accommodating the word, being father to a child, who is the Messiah, Savior, and Redeemer. When Joseph enters the land with the child at the end of chapter 2, Joseph is once again warned in a dream. This time he is told not to go to Jerusalem or Bethlehem, where the son of the evil king reigns now, but rather to go to Nazareth.

Go Down to Egypt

A third parallel in comparing the two Josephs is that they both go down to Egypt. In Genesis 37, the Ishmaelites, who had bought the Old Testament Joseph from his brothers, took him to Egypt and sold him there. In the last chapters of the Book of Genesis, the action takes place predominantly in Egypt, the place out of which the people of God will emerge as slaves freed by the direct intervention of God.

In the New Testament, Matthew writes, "Then Joseph got up, took the child and his mother by night, and went to Egypt and remained there until the death of Herod. This was to fulfil what had been spoken by the Lord through the prophet, 'Out of

Egypt I have called my son'" (Matt 2:14–15). In the citation from the prophet Hosea what is being replayed is the history of Israel, going down to Egypt at the time of Joseph, son of Jacob, in the Old Testament, and then being brought out of Egypt into the land of promise more than four hundred years later.

Fatherhood

A fourth parallel provides another Old Testament light on the New Testament. Joseph in the New Testament is father of Jesus, guardian and protector, playing the role of a father, although he is not a father by natural means. Indeed, of course, he is not a regular father in the biological sense. However, even if it is not the seed of Joseph in Mary's womb, without Joseph there would be no Jesus, for that holy seed of the Spirit would have been swallowed up in the events of a world hostile to the birth and growth of the child. Mary would have been stoned without Joseph to come and take her into his house. Jesus would have been murdered with the innocents in Bethlehem had it not been for Joseph listening closely to the word, and willing to walk in the way of that word by taking the child to Egypt. If he had suddenly stopped listening, they would have stayed in Egypt, a safe place, and never returned to the land where the child must grow and fulfill his mission as Messiah. When they come back to the land, Joseph learns they are not to go to the place where they left from, Bethlehem, or even to Jerusalem, but rather to go to Nazareth. Again and again, the essential role of Joseph is underlined.

At the beginning of Matthew's narrative, when the angel speaks for the first time to Joseph in a dream, he says that Mary will bear a son, and that Joseph is to name him Jesus. Naming is a very significant act in the Old Testament. It is the father who names. This is established in the Book of Genesis, where the first namings of people occur: "This is the list of the descendants of Adam. When God created humankind, he made them in the likeness of God. Male and female he created them, and he blessed them and named them 'Adam' when they were created. When Adam had lived one hundred thirty years, he became the father of a son in his likeness, according to his image, and named him Seth" (Gen 5:1–3). God as father names Adam, and Adam, as father, in turn names Seth. Naming is seen as a paternal act par excellence, and by Joseph naming Jesus, he is manifesting himself as a father. In the modern world, where so many children are born to single mothers, too often abandoned by the men who impregnated them, it is manifest that fathering a child is not defined by biology, by the simple fact of being the source of sperm. Joseph does not contribute his sperm, but he is a model father in Matthew's account. Joseph, who some might call Jesus's "adopted father," is a very real father to a son, Jesus, born into a hostile world. This is also true of many parents who adopt children.

Joseph's fatherhood is paralleled in an indirect way in the story of the Old Testament Joseph. Many Christians might not remember the story of Joseph's sons, Ephraim and Manasseh. In this narrative, a father is rendered "not a father" in the figure of the Old Testament Joseph. Joseph had become a very important man in Egypt, second only to Pharaoh. He had extensive power, and when there was a famine in the land of Canaan, his brothers came to Egypt in search of food. When they came before him, they did not recognize him. After they had sold him, they had told their father that Joseph was dead. Joseph, who was very much alive, would become a savior for them. Joseph's brothers moved down to the land of Egypt, bringing with them their father, Jacob, and Benjamin, Joseph's full brother. Jacob would die in the land of Egypt.

Before Jacob dies, having reached a ripe old age, Joseph hears that Jacob has become weak and feeble. He comes to visit his father to bid him farewell. He brings with him his two sons, born to him in Egypt, Ephraim and Manasseh. As Jacob sits up in his bed to greet this beloved son, who he thought had been killed and has been restored to him, he says, "Your two sons who were born to you in the land of Egypt, before I came to you in Egypt, are now mine. Ephraim and Manasseh shall be mine, just as Reuben and Simeon are. As for the offspring born to you after them, they shall be yours" (Gen 48:5–6). With these words, Jacob makes Joseph a "father who is not a father." Unlike the Joseph of the New Testament, Joseph in the Old Testament has naturally engendered two sons. However, Jacob takes these two sons, Ephraim and Manasseh, as his own, making them equal to his other sons. Jacob has twelve sons, the first two being Reuben and Simeon, the ones he mentions, and the land will be divided among the twelve tribes that descend from these twelve sons. When the land is divided up, two of the sons are not mentioned in the list of tribes—Levi and Joseph. Levi, the tribe of priests, receives no portion of the land, for God is the portion allotted to the Levites. Instead of Joseph, Ephraim and Manasseh are each given portions, restoring the number to twelve.

The parallel between Joseph and Joseph is helpful in understanding these two important characters. Both of them Joseph, son of Jacob; both of them righteous men; both of them playing an essential role in the history of salvation, opening the way of salvation for the people of God. The figure of Joseph, son of Jacob, in the New Testament, is illuminated for readers by the figure of Joseph, son of Jacob, in the Old Testament. This is the way that the New Testament writers write. Almost every word conjures up the Scriptures of Israel. For the God of Israel is the God of Jesus, and the God of Jesus, acting through Jesus, becomes more and more alive in the lives of the readers. What can better reveal who God is than reflecting on the long centuries that precede the coming of Jesus? Matthew begins his story of Jesus with Abraham, the one who enters into a covenant with God. And through all those generations that Matthew cites at the beginning of his narrative, the figure of Joseph, son of Jacob, is undoubtedly a luminous one.

> May we all, men and women,
> be custodians of the child,
> who is the Word of God,
> as Joseph was,
> so that this Word
> might blossom in our embrace,
> and that we might offer the child
> to a world thirsting for God's presence.
> Pray for us, Saint Joseph.

Group Discussion

Refer to the introduction for tips on conducting a group discussion.

Questions for further reflection (select a few questions from the list below that you feel will help stimulate reflection and discussion; you could also use your own questions):

1. What struck you about the parallels between the Joseph of the Old Testament and the Joseph of the New Testament?
2. What did this chapter illuminate for you regarding Joseph's role in Jesus's salvific mission?
3. What did this chapter say to you about Joseph as Jesus's father?
4. Do you agree that God can talk to you in your dreams?
5. Do you listen to God as the two Josephs did, including in your dreams?
6. In what unexpected ways have you been aware of God's message in your life?
7. How has God become more alive to you in these moments?

Chapter 3

Mary the Prophetess

Having looked closely at the figure of Joseph, son of Jacob, the time has come to delve into the figure of Mary. The title of this chapter is "Mary the Prophetess" and hopefully that title will become clear by the end of the chapter.

Mary figures predominantly in the Gospel of Luke. Luke is the evangelist who not only names her but also gives Christians most of what we know about Mary from the New Testament. She is hardly mentioned outside of the books of the Gospel. Among these books, Mark mentions her in two different episodes, but without focusing on her positive role in the life of Jesus. Matthew only mentions her in passing, presenting her as secondary to Joseph. John, without naming her Mary, refers to her as the mother of Jesus, focusing on her at the beginning of Jesus's mission (in Cana of Galilee) and at the end of it (at Jesus's crucifixion in Jerusalem).

In the Gospel according to Mark, probably written before Luke's work and known to him, Mary is mentioned in two problematic contexts. Mark's presentation of Mary is in line with his presentation of Jesus. For Mark, Jesus has emptied himself of his divinity on entering the world, giving up his divinity to be fully human, as described in Paul's hymn in the epistle to the Philippians.

Jesus "emptied himself, taking the form of a slave, being born in human likeness. And being found in human form, he humbled himself and became obedient to the point of death—even death on a cross" (Phil 2:7–8). Jesus's emptying himself of divinity is known as *kenosis*, a Greek word for emptying, and Mary's role in Mark's Gospel highlights this kenosis.

In Mark chapter 3, Jesus's mother, not mentioned by name, sets out with Jesus's brothers to lay their hands on Jesus and stop his mission. They see him as being out of his mind (Mark 3:21). When they find him, they do not go in to him but call him out to them (Mark 3:32). Later, when Jesus is in the synagogue in Nazareth, the explicit mention of Mary, with his brothers and sisters, is a reminder that he is simply a man, and not a very well-regarded one at that: "'Is not this the carpenter, the son of Mary and brother of James and Joses and Judas and Simon, and are not his sisters here with us?' And they took offence at him" (Mark 6:3). In traditional Jewish society, one does not refer to a man by the name of his mother. Referring to Jesus as "the son of Mary" is an insult, implying that his father is unknown. Although Matthew distances himself from this presentation of Mary, he does not focus on her.

Diverging from Mark and Matthew, Luke focuses on Mary as exemplary, a model for every Christian and for the Church as a whole. The Gospel of Luke is a superbly structured text, presenting in its first two chapters a detailed infancy narrative that includes: the Annunciation to Zechariah (1:5–25); the Annunciation to Mary (1:26–38); the Visitation of Mary to Elizabeth (1:39–56); the Birth of John to Elizabeth (1:57–80); and the Birth of Jesus to Mary (2:1–20).

Two Annunciations

There are two annunciations: one to Zechariah, announcing the birth of John the Baptist, and the other to Mary, announcing the birth of Jesus. The parallels between Zechariah and Mary, as well as that between Jerusalem and Nazareth (which is explored in the next chapter) prepare the reader for the parallels between John and Jesus. Zechariah, Jerusalem, and John are surprisingly secondary to Mary, Nazareth, and Jesus—surprisingly, given the priestly status of Zechariah and the importance of Jerusalem in the Old Testament. At the center of chapters 1 and 2 is the meeting of the two pregnant women—Mary and Elizabeth. They both carry in their wombs children who have been conceived in extraordinary circumstances and who meet for the first time in their mothers' wombs, before they are born. One, John, dances in Elizabeth's womb, informing his mother that the other, Jesus, who is arriving in Mary's womb, is her Lord. Finally, there are two fulfillments of the annunciations: first in the birth of John, and then in the birth of Jesus. There are two more narratives in those first two chapters: Jesus at the age of forty days, and Jesus at the age of twelve years, describing the growth and development of the body that is Jesus. This body enters the temple in Jerusalem a first and a second time, preparing for the realization that Jesus is greater than the temple. What Luke describes in chapters 1 and 2 is paralleled in Luke's Acts of the Apostles with the growth and development of the body that represents Jesus in the world—the Church.

Listening Virgin

Beginning his narrative about Mary, Luke writes, "In the sixth month, the angel Gabriel was sent by God to a town in Galilee called Nazareth, to a virgin engaged to a man whose name was Joseph of the house of David. The virgin's name was Mary" (1:26–27). Luke presents Mary immediately following the annunciation to Zechariah. The comparison is thus made, on the one hand, between the two of them. Zechariah is an elderly learned man from the priestly elite, at work in the temple in Jerusalem, who has so much difficulty believing what the angel is telling him as he goes in for the offering of the incense that he leaves the Holy of Holies unable to speak. On the other hand, Mary is a young, simple woman, not in the center in Jerusalem but in a godforsaken place that no one has ever heard of, Nazareth, and she believes immediately and plunges into the adventure that would change her life.

This young woman who is engaged is a virgin. Being a virgin in the Scriptures of Israel does not only evoke a physiological state. The vocabulary of a virgin refers repeatedly to the people of Israel. For Luke, Mary is an ideal representative of the people of Israel, listening closely to the Word of God and obeying. It is in the act of listening closely that she is impregnated. Among the most significant texts in the Scriptures that talk about a virgin are the following:

- Isaiah 37:21–22: "Then Isaiah, son of Amos sent to Hezekiah, saying: 'Thus says the LORD, the God of Israel, because you have prayed to me concerning King Sennacherib of Assyria, this is the word that the LORD has spoken concerning him: she despises you, she scorns you—*virgin daughter Zion*; she tosses her head—behind your back, daughter of Jerusalem.'"
- Jeremiah 18:13: "Therefore thus says the LORD: Ask among the nations: Who has heard the like of this? The *virgin Israel* has done the most horrible thing."
- Jeremiah 31:4: "Again, I will build you, and you shall be built, *O virgin Israel*! Again, you shall take your tambourines, and go forth in the dance of the merrymakers."
  (The reference to taking up tambourines and going forth to dance evokes the dance of Miryam,

sister of Moses, after the people have crossed the
sea and escaped from Pharaoh's armies.)
* Lamentations 2:13: "What can I say for you, to
  what can I compare you, O daughter of Jerusalem?
  To what can I liken you, that I may comfort you,
  O virgin daughter, Zion? For vast as the sea is your
  ruin; who can heal you?"

This word *virgin* that Luke uses to describe Mary is used in
the Old Testament to describe the people of God, the "bride of
God." The virginal state of Israel refers to the people's readiness
to receive the word of God, to hear it and obey it. Unfortunately,
too often this people chooses to listen to other words, prevent-
ing God's word from being received. When this happens, Israel is
referred to as a prostitute in the prophetic texts (most explicitly in
Hos 1:2; Ezek 16:15; Mic 1:7).

In the Christian tradition, another prophetic text is also
included with those that speak of a virgin. It is the text that brings
together a virgin and the child named Immanuel. Isaiah 7:14
reads, "Look, the young woman is with a child and shall bear a
son, and shall name him Immanuel." In the Hebrew version of the
original Isaiah text, the word is *young woman* (in Hebrew *almah*)
and not *virgin*. However, the ancient translation of the Hebrew
into Greek adopted the word *virgin* (*parthenos*)—perhaps not that
surprising, considering that the term *virgin* is used in prophetic
literature in relation to the people of God. In Greek, Isaiah 7:14
reads: "Look, the virgin is with a child and shall bear a son and
you shall name him Immanuel." This verse in Isaiah is taken up
into the Gospel of Matthew, which focuses on Joseph: "All this
took place to fulfil what had been spoken by the Lord through the
prophet" (Matt 1:22). And what has been fulfilled is that Mary is
with child, before she lives with Joseph. The citation is then given:
"'Look, the virgin shall conceive and bear a son, and they shall
name him Immanuel,' which means 'God is with us'" (Matt 1:23).

If Luke is indeed writing after Mark and after Matthew (as many exegetes assume), his description of Mary as "a virgin engaged" echoes not only the prophetic use of the term *virgin* but also the citation of Isaiah 7:14 in its Greek form in the Gospel of Matthew.

In the Book of Isaiah, Immanuel is one of three children mentioned in chapters 7 and 8. A first child is mentioned in Isaiah 7:3. His name is Shear Yeshuv and he is the son of Isaiah, accompanying Isaiah on the way. In Hebrew, the name means "a remnant will return." Later, in chapter 7, the birth of Immanuel is described. It is not clear who the young woman is who is to give birth to a child called Immanuel. Is it the queen, the wife of King Ahaz? This would make the child Hezekiah, a just king and an important figure in the history of Judah. Or is the young woman Isaiah's own wife? Is it simply a young woman passing by in the street under the king's window? She is pregnant at that terrible time of crisis, as the enemy threatens Jerusalem. By confidently carrying new life in her womb, she is incarnating a glimmer of hope on the horizon, ready to bring a child into the world. In her pregnancy, she is presented in stark contrast to King Ahaz, paralyzed by fear.

In chapter 8 of Isaiah, a third child is mentioned. Isaiah says, "And I went to the prophetess, and she conceived and bore a son. Then the LORD said to me, Name him Maher-shalal-hash-baz; for before the child knows how to call 'My father' or 'My mother,' the wealth of Damascus and the spoil of Samaria will be carried away by the king of Assyria" (Isa 8:3-4). The name of this child conjures up war, looting, and destruction, literally meaning "hurry, loot, hasten, spoils." What is particularly interesting is that Isaiah's wife, the woman bearing the child, is termed a prophetess. She is pregnant with a word from God that must be offered as a message to the people.

The three children represent diverse situations in the life of the people with God. Shear Yeshuv, or "a remnant will return," represents God's ultimate fidelity to the promises made to the people. Although destruction will come as a result of the people's infidelity, God's fidelity ensures that a remaining remnant will return from exile and rebuild. The terrible destruction is represented by the name Maher-shalal-hash-baz. However, through it all, it is "Immanuel, God is with us" who represents a present in which God continues to accompany God's people through all the travails. These three children are symbolic signs borne by a prophetess, for she bears these words in her womb and offers them to the world. Understanding these children as being borne by the same woman connects the prophetess to the virgin (young woman) bearing Immanuel.

The Prophetess

In Luke's Gospel, Mary is a virgin. In the Greek text of the New Testament she is named Mariam. It is important to identify the echo this name produces in the Old Testament. Moses's sister in the Pentateuch bears the same name. In Hebrew she is known as *Miryam*, translated into Greek as *Mariam*. Miryam/Mariam/Mary, Moses's sister, plays an important role when the people emerge from the sea, having been saved from Pharaoh's armies.

In Exodus 15, as the people reach the other side of the sea, Miryam is there. This people has emerged from their houses in Egypt, where the doorposts had been splashed with the blood of the Passover lamb. Now they have crossed through the waters of the sea. Blood and water are the signs of a birthing: the people of Israel emerges into the world, on its way to encounter the Father at Sinai. This people had been enslaved, bent over under the burden of Egypt's taskmasters. In a sense, as slaves, they resemble the fetus in the womb. As they emerge from the travail of the blood of the lamb and the water of the sea, Miryam is standing there like a midwife. After the text presents the great song of triumph that Moses sings after the crossing of the sea in Exodus 15, the text continues: "Then the prophetess Miryam, Aaron's sister, took a tambourine in

35

her hand, and all the women went out after her with tambourines and with dancing" (Exod 15:20). The people, bent over in Egypt, are taught to dance by Miryam. They must stand up erect, heads held high, for only thus can they dance. Standing with their heads held high, they can praise the God that Moses has proclaimed as their king. They are no longer slaves to Pharaoh but God's own people.

Miryam's dance is her prophetic response to Moses's song. Her brother proclaimed: "I will sing to the LORD, for he has triumphed gloriously; horse and rider he has thrown into the sea. The LORD is my strength and my might, and he has become my salvation; this is my God, and I will praise him, my father's God, and I will exalt him.... The LORD will reign [will be king] forever and ever" (Exod 15:1–2, 18). Miryam is called a prophet in Exodus 15 not because of words she proclaims but because of her dance, which transforms the people from slaves to free children of God.[1] It is to this experience that Jeremiah refers in the previously quoted text about virgin Israel, "Again, I will build you, and you shall be built, O virgin Israel! Again, you shall take your tambourines, and go forth in the dance of the merrymakers" (Jer 31:4).

With Head Held High

At the center of the Pentateuch, in the Book of Leviticus, there is a beautiful description of this people, standing erect—a free people. It comes at the conclusion of the blessings at the end of the book, in chapter 26. "I am the LORD your God, who brought you out of the land of Egypt to be their slaves no more. I have broken the bars of your yoke and made you walk erect" (Lev 26:13). The word for "walking erect" in Hebrew is *qommemiyut*, and means to walk with your back straight and your head held high—the exact opposite of how slaves walk, bent over. This description of posture, signifying freedom, is an important term for Luke, not so much in his writing of the Jesus story but in his second volume (Acts of the Apostles), which describes the emergence of the Church. The term in Greek used in the rendition of Leviticus 26:13 is *meta parresias*. The role of Miryam (*Mariam* in Greek), the first Mary in the Old Testament, is her taking up of the tambourines so that the people will learn to walk erect, with straight backs and heads held high. This is her prophecy, a prophetic act that envisions a people of slaves becoming a free people. She is there at the moment of birthing.

In the Gospel of Luke, and only there, there is a narrative that resonates with the image of a bent-over slave becoming a free person and walking with head held high. In Luke 13, Jesus, already on his way to Jerusalem, performs very few miracles. Jesus's miracles are concentrated in the chapters about his mission in Galilee (chapters 4–9), which focus on the identity of Jesus. As he walks to Jerusalem (chapters 9–19), most of his teaching is in parables and focuses on who is a disciple. However, there are a few miracles as he walks on the way, and one of them is the healing of a woman bent over, an image of a disciple seeking Jesus so that the disciple can walk erect and enter into the fullness of being with Jesus. Jesus was teaching in a synagogue on the Sabbath when a woman appeared with a spirit that had crippled her for eighteen years. "She was bent over and was quite unable to stand up straight" (13:11). The action continues: "When Jesus saw her, he called her over and said, 'Woman, you are set free from your ailment.' When he laid his hands on her, immediately she stood up straight and began praising God" (13:12–13).

Jesus has to face criticism for performing this miracle on a Sabbath, but he answers those who are protesting: "Ought not this woman, a daughter of Abraham, whom Satan bound for eighteen long years, be set free from this bondage on the sabbath day?" (Luke 13:16). In fact, the spirit that bent her over had prevented this woman from celebrating the Sabbath for eighteen years. The Sabbath is the day that marks both creation and redemption, the exodus from Egypt, the liberation from slavery. Jesus's healing of the woman was not a desecration of the day's holiness but rather a sanctification of the day by freeing the woman to enter the day fully, being restored in the image and likeness of God. The Sabbath ultimately means being able to give thanks for being created in God's image and likeness and for being set free from slavery. It is a day to praise God and dance, celebrating being children of God.

Luke describes the healing as a slave being set free. He does not use the same expression in her regard that is used in Leviticus 26, "walking erect with one's head held high," but the implication is underlined in the description of the woman after the healing: "She stood up straight and began praising God" (13:13). Perhaps the image should be extended: she is dancing, dancing in the synagogue and dancing as she goes home. For the first time in eighteen years, she can celebrate the Sabbath, the day of freedom. However, Luke will use the expression derived from Leviticus 26:13, *meta parresias*—with head held high—repeatedly in Acts of the Apostles.

In the first description of the community in Acts, Mary is present: "All these were constantly devoting themselves to prayer, together with certain women, including Mary the mother of Jesus" (Acts 1:14). Jesus has ascended into heaven, and the community gathers after the apostles had seen him off at the ascension. In the description of the emerging body, at the center of the Church, which is the body that will make Jesus present in the world, Mary is also present, as she is at the conception of Jesus. The body in formation that is the Church must be filled with the Spirit, which will take place at Pentecost. Mary is in fact not only the mother of Jesus, but the mother of the Church, and a symbol of the Church. For the Church too is filled, as she is, with Jesus, and the Church, like Mary, offers him to the world. It is this body, this Church, that walks erect with head held high.

The expression *parresia* is used first in the midst of the Pentecost event. Peter, the head of the community that has just been filled with the Holy Spirit, says: "Fellow Israelites, I may say to you confidently of our ancestor David that he both died and was buried, and his tomb is with us to this day" (Acts 2:29). The Greek expression which is translated "confidently" is precisely that which is derived from Leviticus *meta parresias*—"standing erect with head held high." Peter, head held high, stands erect, fear gone, and speaks out in freedom. He and the others had been slaves to fear: fear of the world that put their master to death, fear of a world that will persecute them because it will not make a place for the gospel that they must announce. The new attitude characterizes the community acting in the Spirit. For example, when Peter addresses the Jewish leaders after his arrest, Acts describes the leaders: "Now when they saw the boldness of Peter and John and realized that they were uneducated and ordinary men, they were amazed and recognized them as companions of Jesus" (4:13). Again the expression translated "boldness" is the one derived from Leviticus 26:13. At the very end of Acts, Paul, under arrest in Rome, is described in these same terms: "He lived there two whole years at his own expense and welcomed all who came to him, proclaiming the kingdom of God and teaching about the Lord Jesus Christ with all boldness and without hindrance" (28:30–31). "With all boldness" is the translation of *meta parresias*. The Spirit has come down to fill the body, and filled with that Spirit, those receiving it can walk erect and hold their heads high. Being filled with the Spirit, as Mary was at the conception of Jesus, they can be like her. It is unfortunate that the translation of the term does not communicate the full image of freedom, joy, and celebration that are rooted in the text of Leviticus 26:13. Now it might make more sense why Luke chooses to end Acts here, as this is the story of the Church—an ongoing story. Luke could not write the ending, because he did not see the end. Even now the Church cannot write the end, for the end is not yet come.

Luke uses the same term in verbal form as well. Barnabas, trying to allay the fears about Saul's past persecution of the community, explains that Saul has been filled with the Spirit: "Barnabas took him, brought him to the apostles, and described for them how on the road he had seen the Lord, who had spoken to him, and how in Damascus he had *spoken boldly* in the name of Jesus. So he went in and out among them in Jerusalem, *speaking boldly* in the name of the Lord" (Acts 9:27–28). The Greek verb *parresia-zomai*, derived from *parresia*, communicates that same posture. The verb is used repeatedly throughout Acts to express the Spirit-imbued way in which the Gospel is preached (Acts 13:46; 14:3; 18:26; 19:8; 26:26).

Mary is a model for the Church and for every Christian. For indeed she has made a place for Jesus at the very center of her life. In this, she is like a prophet who makes place for the word of God at the center of his or her life, willing to be transformed completely by that word. As a "virgin engaged," this was no simple task. Mary might have been put to death for being pregnant before she was joined to her future spouse. Her words, "Let it be with me according to your word" (Luke 1:38), constitute a powerful and prophetic assent to God's plan. Mary is a symbol of the Church, showing us what it means to be filled with the Spirit, pregnant with Jesus, walking with one's head held high. Like Mary, the Church must bear the word of God, standing erect with head held high, and offering Jesus to a world that is waiting.

The Church identifies with Mary each day at evening prayer when the faithful recite the Magnificat, Mary's song when she meets Elizabeth during the Visitation. Her prophetic witness is evident here too, in the Magnificat, in which she sings—again with her head held high—about the overturning of the earthly order.

> He has brought down the powerful from their thrones,
>   and lifted up the lowly;

he has filled the hungry with good things,
   and sent the rich away empty.
He has helped his servant Israel,
   in remembrance of his mercy,
according to the promise he made to our ancestors,
   to Abraham and to his descendants forever.
      (Luke 1:52–55)

Mary's hymn evokes the exodus from slavery and amplifies her voice as a prophetess, one who sees a world liberated from the slavery of our many and diverse pharaohs and who fully embraces the freedom that comes when "my soul magnifies the Lord, and my spirit rejoices in God my Savior" (Luke 1:46–47).

Holy Mary, the Prophetess, pray for us
that we might receive the Child,
that we all, men and women, might be Mothers of God,
mothers of the child who is the Word of God.
Like you, Mary, may we make place for the child in our
   midst,
nurture it and, with heads held high,
offer it to a world thirsting for God's presence.

Group Discussion

Refer to the introduction for tips on conducting a group discussion

Questions for further reflection (select a few questions from the list below that you feel will help stimulate reflection and discussion; you could also use your own questions):

1. Do you listen to and embrace the word of God like Mary at the Annunciation? Or are you also unable to immediately accept God's message, like Zechariah?

2. Are you ready to embrace the word of God unconditionally and allow it to change your life immediately and permanently, as Mary did? What will this mean in your life?

3. Have you ever reflected on Mary as a prophetess? Do you think Luke is underlining Mary's prophetic mission when he describes her as a "virgin engaged"?

4. What comes to mind when you reflect on Mary in the New Testament and Miryam in the Old Testament and their role in helping their communities—the Church and the freed people of Israel—walk, dance, sing, and speak with their heads held high?

5. Describe times you have felt "enslaved, bent over, and burdened" in your life? What helped you to "stand erect, with head held high"?

6. Are you ready to make room to receive the Child who lifts up the lowly and fills the hungry? What will this mean for you?

7. What does it mean to magnify the Lord in your current context and to place Jesus at the center of your life?

Chapter 4

Nazareth and Bethlehem

Jesus is known as the man from Nazareth, but according to Matthew and Luke he was born in Bethlehem. These two towns are not only geographic locations in the story of Jesus but also important indications regarding his identity and mission. They suggest two different aspects through which the Gospel reader can get to know him better. Theologically, Nazareth and Bethlehem represent newness and fulfillment, respectively—two different aspects of Jesus Christ's coming into the world. In this chapter, the discussion will focus first on Nazareth representing newness and then on Bethlehem representing the fulfillment of the old.

The child who is born will come to be known as "Jesus of Nazareth." In John's Gospel, this name is inscribed on the cross when he dies (John 19:19). The first time it is mentioned that Jesus comes from Nazareth is in the first Gospel book that was written, the Gospel of Mark. Mark introduces Jesus at the outset, in the first verse of the book (which might be considered the title): "The beginning of the good news of Jesus Christ, the Son of God" (1:1). In Hebrew, Jesus is "Messiah," or in Greek, "Christ," the anointed one.

He is also Son of God. However, in sharp contrast to these very lofty titles, when Jesus first appears in the narrative, after a description of John the Baptist and his ministry, it is written with audacious simplicity: "In those days Jesus came from Nazareth of Galilee" (Mark 1:9). When Mark writes that Jesus comes from Nazareth, this should come as a shock. This shock is provoked by the fact that Nazareth was never mentioned in the Scriptures of Israel. As far as the Scriptures go, which speak of both Messiah and Son of God, Nazareth is a nonstarter, a nowhere! In the long story of the people of Israel, Nazareth has not been mentioned even once. For a hearer or reader versed in the Scriptures of Israel, what can it mean that the one everyone has been waiting for, the Messiah and the Son of God, comes from a place no one has ever heard of?

Can Anything Good Come out of Nazareth?

The fact that Jesus is known as the man from Nazareth undoubtedly means that Nazareth is indeed the place he came from. No one would have invented this fact, as it certainly does not fit with any theological or scriptural understanding of Jesus as the Christ, the Son of God, the one who fulfills the promises in the Scriptures of Israel. How could he come from nowhere, a place never mentioned in the Scriptures of Israel? An echo of the shock of his origin in Nazareth is found in the Gospel of John. Like Mark, John does not describe Jesus's birth and, as in Mark, Jesus appears right at the beginning at the Jordan River. Shortly after Jesus's baptism in the Jordan, when Jesus is presented by Philip to Nathanael as "him about whom Moses in the law and also the prophets wrote" (John 1:45), Nathanael responds, "Can anything good come out of Nazareth?" (John 1:46). The shock of Jesus being known as the man from Nazareth is repeated later in John's Gospel when people discuss who Jesus is. "Others said,

'This is the Messiah.' But some asked, 'Surely the Messiah does not come from Galilee, does he? Has not the Scripture said that the Messiah is descended from David and comes from Bethlehem, the village where David lived?' So there was a division in the crowd because of him" (7:41–43).

Nazareth is one of the few significant terms in the Gospel that has no echo whatsoever in the Scriptures of Israel, what Christians call the Old Testament. Some, nonetheless, have sought to find an Old Testament echo, however oblique. They have argued that the root of the name Nazareth in Hebrew might be connected to the root of the word *branch* in Hebrew, used in Isaiah 11:1: "A shoot shall come out from the stump of Jesse, and a branch shall grow out of his roots." As attractive as this theory might be because of the Messianic character of the verse, it is farfetched. It ignores the fact that the language the evangelists wrote in was Greek, which was also the language of their audience. In Greek there is no link between the word *Nazareth* and the word *branch*. We don't know whether Matthew knew Hebrew, but there is certainly enough evidence to show that he read the Scriptures in Greek; the version he repeatedly quotes from when citing the Scriptures of Israel is the Septuagint (the ancient Greek translation of the Scriptures). It is highly unlikely, as we will see at the end of this chapter, that even he was making an obscure Hebraic connection between two words that his audience would have been unable to decipher.

In Mark's Gospel, Nazareth comes to signify the radical newness that Mark is chronicling in the life of Jesus. This newness is connected to another word that also has no root in the Old Testament, the word *cross* (*stauros* in Greek). A connection is established between these two words through the fact that there is neither mention of Nazareth nor mention of cross in the ancient Scriptures of Israel. And yet this Jesus, who is Messiah and Son of God, comes from Nazareth and is going to the cross. This is newness, breaking into the old. Of course, without the old, it would be impossible to understand that this is, in fact, newness. The old must be known well in order to identify that there is something new here. Nazareth at the beginning and the cross at the end define the opening and closing parentheses of a life that is stripped of power, the life of a man come to die.

Mark's Gospel, starting with Nazareth and ending at the cross, begins with Jesus's powerful manifestations of his divine power, doing miracle after miracle in Capernaum. From the synagogue cure of the demoniac, the narrative moves to the cure of Simon Peter's mother-in-law and then to the cure of many, both physically and mentally ill, after the Sabbath ends. However, the story Mark must tell is not one of a powerful hero but of a crucified criminal. This is integral to the newness that emerges as he writes of Jesus moving from Nazareth to the cross, emptying himself of the power and authority that seem to characterize him at the beginning of the narrative but of which he is stripped at the end.

Kenosis: Jesus Empties Himself

Mark's writing evokes Paul's powerful description of Jesus emptying himself in Philippians 2:5–11. According to Paul, the believer is to follow Jesus as a disciple, being of the same mind as Jesus was. The emptying that takes place when Jesus comes into the world is described step by step: Jesus empties himself of divine mastery, of power, of everything that he might be in his oneness with God, when he becomes a human person, a slave who dies on the cross. This emptying is known as *kenosis*, from the Greek verb used in Paul's text. It is through his obedient death on the cross that he is then glorified by God:

> Let the same mind be in you that was in Christ Jesus,
> who, though he was in the form of God,
>> did not regard equality with God as something to be
>> exploited,

but emptied himself,
> taking the form of a slave,
> being born in human likeness.

And being found in human form,
> he humbled himself
> and became obedient to the point of death—
> even death on a cross.

Therefore, God also highly exalted him
> and gave him the name
> that is above every name,

so that at the name of Jesus
> every knee should bend,
> in heaven and on earth and under the earth,

and every tongue should confess
> that Jesus Christ is Lord,
> to the glory of God the Father. (Phil 2:5–11)

Mark's adoption of this "kenotic theology" is already hinted at when he underlines that Jesus is coming from Nazareth (1:9) after he has proclaimed that Jesus is Messiah and Son of God (1:1). It is the beginning of the way to the cross.

Bethlehem's Deep Connection to the History of Salvation

There is, however, a sharp distinction between the Gospel accounts of Mark and John on the one hand, and those of Matthew and Luke on the other. Mark and John have no infancy narratives and first present Jesus as a fully grown man, beginning their presentations at the Jordan. Matthew and Luke, each in their own way, begin their presentations with the infant Jesus. In these two accounts, Bethlehem plays a central role. Unlike Nazareth, Bethlehem is a well-known place that is deeply connected to the history of salvation, the place expected to be at the origin of the Messiah.

In Matthew, Bethlehem is introduced as the place where Jesus was born. Matthew does not focus on the moment of Jesus's birth. Rather he describes that, at the time Jesus was born, men came from the East, led by a star. These men represent the Gentiles and conjure up figures from both the Book of Psalms and the Book of Isaiah. "May the kings of Tarshish and of the isles render him tribute, may the kings of Sheba and Seba bring gifts" (Ps 72:10). "A multitude of camels shall cover you, the young camels of Midian and Ephah; all those from Sheba shall come. They shall bring gold and frankincense, and shall proclaim the praise of the LORD" (Isa 60:6). Those coming, representing the nations, are seeking the light that radiates from Israel, as Israel has been called to be a light to the nations.

Matthew introduces a star into his narrative. These men from the nations are not familiar with the revelation God has entrusted to the people of Israel in the Scriptures. Israel has no need to search for the way in which to live, for God has revealed that way in the gift of the Torah. However, God does not abandon the nations, leaving them without a way to discover that there is a God who has ordered all things. Although they do not have Torah, they do have nature, the created world—a world that, when wisely meditated upon, can reveal the Creator God and how they should live in conformity with God's will. This is the way of wisdom, for the nations' wisdom is parallel to Torah for the Jews. Nature, in the form of the star, leads the men toward the child.

However, the star does not take them from the East directly to Bethlehem where Jesus has been born. It takes them first to Jerusalem. This is a surprising aspect of the narrative. While wisdom orients, only revelation achieves its end. Matthew insists that these Gentiles must encounter the Jewish people and their Scriptures before they can come to the Messiah. In Jerusalem, to which the star leads them, they come before the king, Herod, who is surrounded by his sages. The question the wise men then pose to the king in Jerusalem is shocking: "Where is the child who has been born king of the Jews? For we observed his star at its rising, and have come to pay him homage" (2:2). They have come before the king, and they ask, Where is the king? This is what provokes the enormous consternation that seizes Herod and all around him. These wise men are underlining the fact that Herod is not the real king of Israel.

The Real King of Israel

The real king of Israel is God, manifest in that child newly born. This is what is supposed to characterize the people of God. From the moment the people emerged from Egyptian slavery, having crossed the sea, Moses sings, "The LORD reigns forever" (Exod 15:18). Unlike other peoples, this people must bear witness to the kingship of God. King Herod understands perfectly what the men from the East are referring to, and he trembles with fear. This human flesh-and-blood king is going to be challenged by the king of Israel who has now been born.

The men ask the king where they can find the newborn king. It is this that they must learn from the Jews and their Scriptures. The star has led them to the Jewish center and once they find out where Jesus is born, the star will continue to lead them to the child. Matthew describes Herod's reaction: "Calling together all the chief priests and scribes of the people, he inquired of them where the Messiah was to be born" (2:4). Herod has understood that they are talking about the true king, the Messiah. His scribes and chief priests tell him, quoting from the prophet Micah, "In Bethlehem of Judea; for so it has been written by the prophet: And you, Bethlehem, in the land of Judah are by no means least among the rulers of Judah; for from you shall come a ruler who is to shepherd my people Israel." (Matt 2:4–6 quoting Mic 5:2). Matthew's unique infancy narrative focuses on the fulfillment of

God's promises in the coming of Jesus into the world. The quotation from Micah about Bethlehem is the second of five scriptural references which Matthew insists are fulfilled in Jesus's appearance. Unlike Mark, Matthew insists on the fulfillment of the old, not only on newness. What is at stake is not only the newness represented by Nazareth, but the old as fulfillment of prophecy, represented by Bethlehem.

Bethlehem represents important moments in the long history of salvation, making numerous appearances in the Scriptures of Israel. Bethlehem is mentioned for the first time in Genesis, being the place where Rachel is buried (35:19). Rachel, the beloved wife of the last of the patriarchs, Jacob, died giving birth. Much further along in the history of salvation, there is a focus on Bethlehem at the end of the Book of Judges. Judges, the seventh book of the Old Testament, tells the story, not of Israel's fidelity to the word, but rather Israel's descent into darkness and sin. In the first part of Judges, in chapters 1 to 16, there are twelve cycles of Israel descending into the darkness of sin, resulting in the chaotic triumph of the nations over Israel. Twelve times the people are crushed by hostile nations. Twelve times they cry out in their suffering and God sends them twelve judges, military leaders and rulers, to save them from the nations. While the military ruler lives (the most important of them being Gideon) the people remain faithful. But as soon as the ruler dies, Israel once again descends into darkness. When Gideon dies, having refused to be king, his bastard son, Abimelech, seizes power, makes himself king and brings Israel again into profound darkness.

The last five chapters of the Book of Judges are among the most horrific chapters in the Bible: five chapters of total darkness. There is no salvation. Israel, in its sinfulness, has exiled God from its own story. This reads like a repetition of the sin of Adam and Eve and the cycles of sin that followed (Gen 3—11). Israel descends into sins of idolatry and prostitution, civil war and murder. As darkness obliterates the light that had been at the center of the Book of Joshua as the people entered the land, a refrain is heard over and over again. Four times the author insists that in those days "there was no king in Israel." Although this is literally the case, referring to a time before the kings ruled in Israel, that is, before the days of Saul, David, and Solomon, the refrain also refers to the vocation of Israel that has been betrayed. Israel is supposed to be the one nation that points to God as its king, and yet they have turned their backs on God. Israel, distinct from other nations, should have God as king and not a flesh-and-blood alternative, a king who would inevitably become a tyrant, who would think of himself as God—a king like Herod.

The refrain at the end of Judges, "In those days there was no king in Israel" (21:25; cf. 17:6; 18:1; 19:1), points to the darkness that has enveloped the nation. Sin has been victorious, death and darkness have vanquished; must God's plan now be abandoned? Absolutely not! What is important to note in these five chapters detailing the descent into darkness is that Bethlehem plays a central role. The sins of idolatry, prostitution, murder, and civil war originate time and again in Bethlehem. The Levite priest who comes to lead worship in the idolatrous household of Micah comes from Bethlehem (Judg 17:7–9). The concubine whose brutal murder sets off the events that plunge Israel into civil war comes from Bethlehem (19:1–2). The end of these bloodcurdling sagas is the repetition of the refrain in the final verse of the book regarding the absence of a king in Israel, meaning that God does not dwell in the midst of the people called to be a light to the nations. The people called to be a light is a people plunged in darkness.

Ruth Transforms Bethlehem into an Oasis of Light

In the Christian canon of the Old Testament, the Book of Ruth is the next book after Judges. It begins with the words that link it to Judges, "In the days when the judges judged" (Ruth 1:1). There is a radical shift of perspective in this book. From the focus on the people of Israel in the land of Israel, the focus turns to Ruth, not a member of the people of Israel, living in the land of Moab. Ruth being a Moabite means that she belongs to a people that Israel abhors, a people vilified in the Old Testament. The Moabites and the neighboring Ammonites were seen as the descendants of the incestuous union between Lot and his two daughters, after the destruction of Sodom, Gomorrah, and the other cities in the time of Abraham (Gen 19:37–38). Later, when the people emerged from Egypt, the Moabites and the Ammonites are described as those who refused to welcome Israel as the people passed by. In the law given to Israel, the Moabites and the Ammonites were destined for eternal damnation, never to be part of God's people (Deut 23:3–4).

Yet, the Book of Ruth presents a surprising contradiction to the law. Ruth is married to an Israelite, joining a family from the people of Israel that had moved into Moab, abandoning the land of Israel. After the death of her husband, Ruth will accompany her mother-in-law, Naomi, who has been widowed and has lost both her sons. In an act of self-sacrificing love, she accompanies her on her way back to her homeland, to the town of her birth, to Bethlehem. Naomi tries to dissuade Ruth, saying that she should go back to her own people. However, Ruth turns to her mother-in-law and says, "Where you go, I will go; where you lodge, I will lodge; your people shall be my people, and your God my God. Where you die, I will die—there will I be buried" (Ruth 1:16–17). Ruth the Moabite, instead of facing eternal damnation as proposed by the law for Moabites, moves into the orbit of Israel, bringing her light of fidelity to her mother-in-law and her light of faith in the God of her mother-in-law.

Ruth is a luminous example of faith, following in the footsteps of Abraham who went from his land, from his tribe, from his father's house to a land that God showed him. At the end of the

Book of Ruth, she will be identified as the great-grandmother of King David. Bethlehem, a place of profound darkness in Judges, has become an oasis of light in Ruth. It will become known as the City of David, the king that emerges from that place. In the Gospel of Matthew, in the genealogy that introduces Jesus, Ruth is remembered: "Salmon, the father of Boaz by Rahab, and Boaz the father of Obed by Ruth" (Matt 1:5–6). In this part of Matthew's genealogy, Ruth stands alongside Rahab the Canaanite, presented here as her second mother-in-law, she too a surprising woman of faith.

In Matthew's narrative, the wise men go out from the presence of the king, who orders them to come back and tell him when they have found the child. Herod claims that he also wants to go and worship the newborn king. The star continues to lead the wise men to the place where Jesus is lying in Bethlehem. They find the child, worship, and leave their gifts. Then, in a dream, the men from the nations (like Joseph, the man of dreams open to the Word of God) are warned not to go back to Herod. Although they are not from Israel, they are presented as also being open to the word that comes to them from on high. They do not go back, because they realize that Herod, like many kings of this world, is a "pharaoh." Indeed, he intends to wipe out the child. He will wipe out many, many children, but Joseph saves the child, Jesus.

Unlike Mark, Matthew places the birth of Jesus in Bethlehem. However, he cannot ignore the embarrassing fact that Jesus is the man from Nazareth and not referred to as Jesus of Bethlehem. At the end of his infancy narrative, he must deal with Nazareth. In the fifth and last narrative that constitutes this infancy gospel, Joseph continues to listen carefully to the voices in his dreams so that he can fulfill the Word in his role as Jesus's father. He hears the call to go back to the land of Israel, but it comes with a warning: do not go to Jerusalem, for the son of that evil king is ruling in Jerusalem, and he might do the child harm. The call is to go to Nazareth. But Nazareth is presented in strikingly strange terms:

"There he made his home in a town called Nazareth, so that what had been spoken through the prophets might be fulfilled, 'He will be called a Nazarene'" (Matt 2:23). Matthew writes that Nazareth fulfills what the "prophets" had spoken. The formula "so that what had been spoken through the prophets might be fulfilled" makes this fifth narrative parallel to the four that had preceded it, all of them embroidered around a verse from the prophets that had been fulfilled. In the first four narratives a prophet had spoken— Isaiah (1:22–23), Micah (2:5–6), Hosea (2:15), and Jeremiah (2:17–18)—and Jesus's coming into the world fulfilled the easily identifiable prophetic word. However, in this final narrative, the supposed prophetic word is unidentifiable: "He will be called a Nazarene." That is written nowhere in the prophetic writings of Israel.

Out of Nothing, God Brings Everything

Matthew offers a clue that this is not simply a citation because he prefaces the citation with "the prophets" in plural. He seems to be saying that a collection of prophets spoke something that is fulfilled in Jesus: he will be called a man of Nazareth. However, there is no Nazareth in the Old Testament, so what can Matthew mean when he says "the prophets" spoke of a man from Nazareth?

This has long been recognized as a difficult exegetical problem. Perhaps the solution is found in what was suggested earlier: Nazareth represents nothingness, formlessness, and invisibility. What Matthew might mean when he alludes to all the prophets is that they all affirm that out of nothing, God can bring everything! This is the radical newness of God. In fact, this is underlined right from the beginning of Scripture. God has brought everything out of the formlessness and invisibility of nothingness. "In the beginning when God created the heavens and the earth, the earth was a formless void and darkness covered the face of the deep" (Gen 1:1–2). It is this newness and creativity that is proclaimed by all the prophets. This creation out of nothingness is newness, parallelled in the resurrection from the dead. It constitutes the ever-surprising activity of God who alone can bring everything from nothingness, life from death, the Messiah and Son of God from Nazareth. God does not act according to a preconceived recipe. It is not that God has a book and follows instructions. Even out of Nazareth, never mentioned in the Scriptures of Israel, God can bring the fullness of accomplishment.

Matthew is pointing to this reality when he declares that Jesus is from Nazareth, and that this fulfills what all the prophets have said. For indeed they have said that God will make new; God will bring newness, new heavens, and a new earth. The nothingness of Nazareth indeed parallels the nothingness of the cross and from this nothingness God brings the fulness of life—his Son, the risen Messiah. At the center of Matthew's Gospel, at the end of the third of the five great discourses of Jesus that characterize the book, after speaking of the parables, Jesus says, "Therefore, every scribe who has been trained for the kingdom of heaven is like the master of a household who brings out of his treasure what is new and what is old" (Matt 13:52). Jesus draws attention to the treasure of both old and new: the new represented by Nazareth, and the old represented by Bethlehem.

Many exegetes believe that Mark was the first Gospel book that was written. Matthew, based firmly on Mark's account, composed his Gospel after Mark. In Mark, focusing on radical newness, there is no mention of Bethlehem. Jesus is Jesus of Nazareth, a fact that Mark understands theologically as kenotic—Jesus emptying himself, emerging from the nothingness of Nazareth. Matthew firmly places the birth of Jesus in Bethlehem, even though he has to deal with the fact that Jesus is from Nazareth. Whereas Mark might be considered the Gospel of newness, Matthew might be considered the Gospel of fulfillment of the old.

The Old Gives Way to the New

What does Luke, the third synoptic evangelist (who, like Matthew, places Jesus's birth in Bethlehem) add concerning the question of Nazareth? In the first chapter of Luke, the beginning of his infancy narrative, there are two annunciations: the annunciation to Zechariah and the annunciation to Mary. The first, the one to Zechariah, takes place at the center of the history of salvation: in Jerusalem, in the temple, in the Holy of Holies. Zechariah is a priest, an old man, who has spent a long life of fidelity to the law. He is childless, and that is a great sorrow for him. In their childlessness, Zechariah and his wife Elizabeth evoke the greatest of the patriarchs, Abraham, and his wife, Sarah. As he serves in the temple, an angel appears to him: "Then there appeared to him an angel of the Lord standing at the right side of the altar of incense" (Luke 1:11). The angel announces the forthcoming birth of a son, John the Baptist. However, this narrative is pointing to someone who is coming who is greater than John. Zechariah is completely astounded and finds it hard to believe, and he emerges from the Holy of Holies struck dumb to rejoin Elizabeth.

The second annunciation takes place in Nazareth: "In the sixth month, the angel Gabriel was sent by God to a town in Galilee, called Nazareth" (1:26). This time the recipient of the angel's message is a young, inexperienced woman, in a totally marginal place, a place of nothingness called Nazareth. She receives the annunciation that she will be the mother, not of a prophet, but the mother of the Son of God, whom she will carry in her womb. The newness that Luke is proposing is explicit in the parallel between Zechariah and Mary: the old man, who is a member of the priestly elite, venerable and admirable (albeit incredulous), is about to father a child who will be the greatest of prophets, John the Baptist; whereas the simple village girl is to carry in her womb the Son of God, in astounding obedience and faith. Luke, however, is not only comparing Mary with Zechariah, the old priest with the young girl, he is also overshadowing Jerusalem with the newness that is Nazareth.

In a certain sense, out of the nothingness of Nazareth, the fulfillment of all emerges because of Mary's prophetic yes to be the one who bears Jesus, thus giving him to the world. Her womb, in which there is no seed of life, prefigures the tomb, in which there is no life. From her womb emerges the child who is awaited, and from the tomb emerges, just as surprisingly, the one who puts death to death, the manifestation of the victory of life in the resurrection. Luke has taken Matthew's theology of the new and the old a step further by declaring that the new will be even greater than the old. This is not in contradiction with what the prophets proclaimed in the Old Testament, for there it is expected that the old will indeed give way to the new. In the aftermath of the nothingness of the exile, when everything had been reduced to ruins, Isaiah could affirm: "For I am about to create new heavens and a new earth; the former things shall not be remembered or come to mind. But be glad and rejoice forever in what I am creating; for I am about to create Jerusalem as a joy, and its people as a delight" (Isa 65:17–18).

> As we prepare
> to receive the child,
> may we all be able to both honor the old
> and receive the newness that is promised in the child who
>   bursts into the world.
>
> May our arms be open to embrace this child
> and offer the child to a world thirsting for God's presence.
> Pray for us, holy Mary, mother of God.
> Pray for us, Saint Joseph, father of Jesus.
> Pray for us, Saint Ruth, astonishing woman of faith.
> Pray for us, Saint David, king and singer of God's praises.
> Amen.

Group Discussion

Refer to the introduction for tips on conducting a group discussion

Questions for further reflection (select a few questions from the list below that you feel will help stimulate reflection and discussion; you could also use your own questions):

1. How do you respond to the idea that Jesus, the Son of God, has effectively come from "nowhere" given that Nazareth has no echo in the Scriptures of Israel?
2. Does this realization amplify in any way the self-emptying, or kenosis, that Paul describes in his letter to the Philippians?
3. In what way must we undergo a "kenosis" or an emptying in our lives to receive the Word of God?
4. How do you understand the following text in Paul's letter to the Philippians? "Let the same mind be in you that was in Christ Jesus, who, though he was in the form of God, did not regard equality with God as something to be exploited, but emptied himself, taking the form of a slave, being born in human likeness and being found in human form, he humbled himself and became obedient to the point of death—even death on a cross." What might this mean for you in your life at the moment?
5. What struck you about the star and the role of nature in leading the wise men from the nations to Jesus? Do you believe nature can lead us to the Creator God? In what ways can we allow nature to lead us to God?
6. Do you agree that Nazareth points to the newness of Jesus, while Bethlehem represents the fulfillment of prophecy?
7. What do you take from the way Ruth, an outsider to the people of Israel, plays a central role in turning Bethlehem (regarded as a place of darkness and sin in Judges) into an oasis of light?
8. If Nazareth represents nothingness, formlessness, and invisibility, what does it say to you about God's transformative power to create everything out of nothing?
9. Do you think the nothingness of Nazareth parallels the nothingness of the cross? Does this change your understanding of the gospel? In what way?
10. In your own life, are you willing to allow the old to give way to the new, while still honoring the old? In what way?

Chapter 5

Jesus: A Child Is Born

Haying looked closely at Jesus's ancestors, the figure of Joseph in the Gospel of Matthew, the figure of Mary in the Gospel of Luke, and at Nazareth and Bethlehem in all four books of the Gospel, our focus now turns to Jesus himself as he is presented in the infancy narratives. In this chapter, attention is focused on the single verse that describes his birth.

A Christmas Icon

There is only one verse in the New Testament that describes the Christmas moment, the moment the child is born. It is found in the Gospel of Luke. "She gave birth to her firstborn son and wrapped him in bands of cloth, and laid him in a manger, because there was no place for them in the inn" (Luke 2:7). This verse not only gives information about the birth of the child; it is also a true icon that delivers layers of meaning to explain who this child is and what fate awaits him.

The pronoun *she* refers to Mary, the central figure in Luke's infancy narrative. She is the subject of the three verbs that follow.

She gave birth, wrapped him, and laid him—three verbs carried out by the Mary identified earlier as a prophetess. The reader is invited to be surprised, perhaps even shocked, that the child is laid in a manger. This is a place for food for animals, not the place to lay a newborn child. Luke explains this anomaly by saying there was no place in "the inn." The translation of the Greek term corresponding to the expression "inn" is not completely satisfactory within the context of Luke's Gospel or the echoes the Greek term evokes in the Old Testament. This word will be further explored later in the chapter. However, the structure of the verse is clear: three actions are performed, followed by a negative explanation "no place."

Luke repeats exactly this structure—three verbs and a negative appendix—in another verse toward the end of his Gospel. Hearing these two verses alongside one another drives home the similarity in the cadences of the two verses.

> She gave birth to her firstborn son and wrapped him in bands of cloth, and laid him in a manger, because there was no place for them in the inn. (2:7)

> He took it down, and wrapped it in a linen cloth, and laid it in a rock-hewn tomb where no one had ever been laid. (23:53)

The subject of the second verse, with its three verbs and its negative appendix, is Joseph of Arimathea. The magnificence of the rhythmic quality of these two verses read side by side characterizes Luke's writing. The object of the verbs in both verses is the body of Jesus. The first verse describes his body's emergence into the world at his birth, while the second verse describes his body's exit from the world at his burial. The first prepares for the second; the second sheds light on the first.

In his own way, Matthew also links Jesus's entry into the world with his exit from it. When the three men come from the

East to worship the child, they bring gifts that echo the Old Testament in Isaiah 60. "A multitude of camels shall cover you, the young camels of Midian and Ephah; all those from Sheba shall come. They shall bring gold and frankincense, and shall proclaim the praise of the LORD" (Isa 60:6). Matthew describes the men's arrival in Bethlehem. "On entering the house, they saw the child with Mary his mother; and they knelt down and paid him homage. Then, opening their treasure chests, they offered him gifts of gold, frankincense, and myrrh" (Matt 2:11). Among their gifts, the gold (for a king) and the frankincense (for a priest) resonate with the text in Isaiah. However, myrrh is a surprise. It also points to the destiny of this king and priest, this Messiah: a surprise that is revealed on the Sunday after his death and burial. The women bearing myrrh seek him in the tomb to prepare his body, because there had been no time to do that before the Sabbath, the day he had died.

It is interesting to note that in traditional Byzantine iconography (such as the image on the cover of this book) there is a further feature derived from the Lukan nativity verse. The baby wrapped in bands of cloth is not represented as a baby in diapers, an impression that might be given by a literal understanding of Mary's wrapping the baby. Rather, the baby looks like it has already been enshrouded in the burial cloth that is explicitly mentioned in the description of the act of Joseph of Arimathea. This too hints at the prophetic nature of Mary's action.

Firstborn Son

Luke, like all the other Gospel writers, counts heavily on the reader's familiarity with the Scriptures of Israel. The expression "firstborn son" carries strong Old Testament echoes. It is the "firstborn son" that is called out of Egypt. When God first meets Moses in the burning bush, God says to Moses: "Thus says the LORD:

Israel is my firstborn son. I said to you, 'Let my son go that he may worship me.' But you refused to let him go; now I will kill your firstborn son" (Exod 4:22–23). Matthew uses another reference to Israel's sonship as a prefiguration of Jesus's own sonship with a citation from the prophet Hosea: "When Israel was a child, I loved him, and out of Egypt I called my son" (Hos 11:1, cf. Matt 2:15), which, according to Matthew, is fulfilled in Jesus's descent into Egypt, fleeing Herod. Jeremiah uses the same expression found in Luke—"firstborn." Interestingly, however, in Jeremiah the context is not the Exodus from Egypt but the return from the Babylonian exile.

> See, I am going to bring them from the land of the north, and gather them from the farthest parts of the earth, among them the blind and the lame, those with child and those in labor, together; a great company, they shall return here. With weeping they shall come, and with consolations I will lead them back, I will let them walk by brooks of water, in a straight path in which they shall not stumble; for I have become a father to Israel, and Ephraim is my firstborn. (Jer 31:8–9)

The term used by Luke is "firstborn son," which is a significant term in the Scriptures of Israel. This does not necessarily mean that Mary had other children. Catholics would insist that Jesus is her only son and that the brothers and sisters of Jesus mentioned in the books of the Gospel were not hers (cf. Mark 3:31–32, 6:3 and parallels). However, it should be pointed out that the term "firstborn son" implies something very important about the identity and mission of Jesus Christ. God wants Jesus to be the firstborn son with many brothers and sisters who believe in him and walk in his way. In the Letter to the Hebrews, it is written,

It was fitting that God, for whom and through whom all things exist, in bringing many children to glory, should make the pioneer of their salvation perfect through sufferings. For the one who sanctifies and those who are sanctified all have one Father. For this reason, Jesus is not ashamed to call them brothers and sisters, saying, "I will proclaim your name to my brothers and sisters, in the midst of the congregation I will praise you." (Heb 2:10–12)

Jesus is God's "only Son" because he is the only one who remains completely faithful to the Father, the only one without sin. The unique character of Jesus's being the only Son, as liturgical formulae often repeat, does not fill God's heart with joy, for God wishes Jesus to be the firstborn of a great multitude who can say with Jesus, "Our Father."

The Manger

The reader of Luke's nativity is undoubtedly invited to notice that it is strange to place an infant in a manger. However, the Old Testament echo is a powerful insight into the nativity of the child Jesus. At the beginning of the book of Isaiah, the prophet bewails the sad spiritual state of the people who have turned away from their God. "The ox knows its owner, and the donkey its master's manger; but Israel does not know, my people do not understand" (Isa 1:3). In the Greek version of Isaiah, the one familiar to the New Testament writers, the word used for what the donkey must understand, the manger, is the same word Luke uses for the place where Mary lays her child. Isaiah's pain at the spiritual state of the people of God is echoed in Luke's use of the image of the manger.

The ox and the donkey mentioned in Isaiah's verse have become an integral part of the traditional nativity scene set up by so many Christians in preparation for Christmas. The scene is often attributed to Saint Francis but can already be distinguished in the traditional iconography of the Byzantine Church, where the ox and the ass are seen alongside the manger. The roots of the image, however, are in the Old Testament and its evocation in the New Testament. Luke, like so many of the New Testament writers, is confronted with what Paul refers to as the mystery of the incredulity of the people of Israel faced with the coming of the Messiah, the Son of God. "So that you may not claim to be wiser than you are, brothers and sisters, I want you to understand this mystery: a hardening has come upon part of Israel, until the full number of the Gentiles has come in" (Rom 11:25).

Jesus's Birth and the Last Supper

Mary laid the child in a manger because there was no place in "the inn." The Greek term translated in the New Revised Standard Version of the Bible as "inn" is another of those words that has profound Old Testament echoes. However, before examining these echoes to understand more profoundly Mary's prophetic action and Jesus's Messianic identity, it is important to note that Luke makes one more use of this word in his writings. Luke wrote fifty-two of the chapters in the New Testament. This means that he composed about one quarter of the entire New Testament—the twenty-four chapters of his book of the Gospel and the twenty-eight chapters of the Acts of the Apostles. However, he uses this specific Greek word only twice, undoubtedly wanting the reader to connect the two occurrences of the word. Unfortunately, due to the inconsistency of translation, the connection intended by the author is obscured because the identity of the two words is not preserved in translation. These two verses should also be read side by side:

> She gave birth to her firstborn son and wrapped him in bands of cloth, and laid him in a manger, because there was no place for them in the *inn*. (2:7)

> Say to the owner of the house, "The teacher asks you, 'Where is the *guest room*, where I may eat the Passover with my disciples?'" (22:11)

In this translation, the parallel is not apparent because of the two disparate words used to translate the single Greek term. The Greek word *kataluma* (κατάλυμα) is used in both 2:7 and 22:11, and only in these two places in Luke's writings. It is translated by two different terms in English, *inn* and *guest room*. The precise translation of the term *kataluma* is difficult to pin down and will be discussed when the echoes in the Old Testament are identified.

The second use of *kataluma* in chapter 22 of Luke's Gospel reveals much about the significance of its use in Luke's description of Jesus's birth in chapter 2. In chapter 22, Jesus sends two of his disciples ahead of the rest to Jerusalem to prepare the place where they will celebrate the Passover. As they set off, he says to them, "Listen, when you have entered the city, a man carrying a jar of water will meet you; follow him into the house he enters and say to the owner of the house, 'The teacher asks you, where is the guest room [*kataluma*], where I may eat the Passover with my disciples?' He will show you a large room upstairs, already furnished. Make preparations for us there" (22:10–12). Whereas the *kataluma* was not ready for Jesus at his birth, it is now furnished and ready.

The Passover meal in the *kataluma* is particularly significant for the description of Jesus's birth. The *kataluma* is ready for the celebration of the Passover. What happens during the Passover meal that Jesus, the night before he will be crucified, celebrates with his disciples? This is the feast of the liberation from slavery in Egypt, the commemoration of God's decisive action in favor of God's firstborn son, the people of Israel. It is during this meal that Jesus takes the unleavened bread and says, "This is my body, which is given for you. Do this in remembrance of me" (22:19). Jesus institutes the Eucharistic meal at this moment, the meal that sustains the Church, the Body of Christ, preparing for his coming at the end of time. With the words pronounced in the *kataluma*, Christ's ongoing presence in the Church is guaranteed.

What is remarkable in Luke's composition is the connection he is making using the word *kataluma* in the preparation for the Last Supper, the Passover meal, and Jesus's birth. Mary, the prophetess, laid him in a manger at his birth. This is no longer a curiosity. It is a prophetic act. She lays her baby in a place that is meant for food. Jesus, the night before he is crucified, gives himself as food, as bread. John, in his book of the Gospel, which has no description of the Last Supper, has Jesus say, "I am the bread of life" (John 6:35). Mary the prophetess lays her child in a manger, offering him to a hungry world that wants the bread of life. The child who is born is the bread of life, laid in a manger.

How should the word *kataluma* be translated? Most importantly, however it is translated, verse 2:7 and 22:11 must use the same word in order to show the connection between the two verses. However, tracing back the word into the Old Testament, the task of choosing a unitary term for the Greek word becomes even more complicated. It is important to remember that the Old Testament version that must be consulted is the Septuagint, the ancient Greek version, the version used by the New Testament authors. The word *kataluma* does not appear with great regularity in the Septuagint. Nonetheless, there is a very important text, a text that regularly echoes throughout Luke's Gospel.

In chapter 7 of 2 Samuel, King David, at the peak of his

power, has built himself a magnificent house, a palace befitting a king. "Now when the king was settled in his house, and the LORD had given him rest from all his enemies around him, the king said to the prophet Nathan, 'See now, I am living in a house of cedar, but the ark of God stays in a tent'" (2 Sam 7:1–2). The king here is David, the beloved of God, the one who loves God and whom God loves (the root of the name David in Hebrew is the word *love* in Hebrew). God has given David rest from all his enemies. The term *rest* employed here prefigures an eschatological (end of time) rest that will come at the end of history. However, David then falls into the trap of kings of flesh and blood. The king has built himself a magnificent house, a royal palace, as is the way of kings in this world. This is not in itself a sin. However, when he looks out of the window and he sees the "tent of meeting" (or as Luke would have read in the Greek "the tent of witness"), he is shocked. This tent, in which God dwells, is not a royal palace but a tent. David is living in a magnificent house and God is living in a tent. David's desire to build a fitting house for God, a temple, seems to intimate that David seeks a God in his image and likeness. His God should also dwell in a palace, like David does.

Nathan, who is the prophet in David's court, becomes a false prophet when he says to the king, "Go, do all that you have in mind; for the LORD is with you" (2 Sam 7:3). He is a false prophet because he answers David without consulting God, for whom he, as a prophet, is supposed to be the spokesperson. However, the sin might even be graver than that. David, who seeks to create a God in his image, a God who dwells in a palace like he does, seems to be regarded as God by Nathan, who simply approves of David's intention, speaking back David's word to David rather than consulting God.

The narrative continues with God's own entrance into the story. "But that same night the word of the LORD came to Nathan: Go and tell my servant David: Thus says the LORD" (2 Sam 7:4–5).

God sets things straight. The prophet is a person who steps into the crisis of communication between God and humanity. The prophet is a necessary mediator when communication breaks off because of sin. Nathan, who had fallen short in the initial encounter with David, is now called to carry a divine message to David, thus fulfilling his role as prophet. The message Nathan is called to communicate is a slap in the face for David: God does not want a house, a palace, or a temple.

Kataluma: The Place of God's Presence

God's words, delivered to David through Nathan, are:

Are you the one to build me a house to live in? I have not lived in a house since the day I brought up the people of Israel from Egypt to this day, but I have been moving about in a tent and a tabernacle. Wherever I have moved about among all the people of Israel, did I ever speak a word with any of the tribal leaders of Israel, whom I commanded to shepherd my people Israel, saying, "Why have you not built me a house of cedar?" (2 Sam 7:5–7)

God does not want a house that pins God down, rather God moves about "in a tent and a tabernacle." In this expression, which defines the very place of God's presence, the term *kataluma* is to be found as the equivalent for the word *tent* in the Hebrew text. The *kataluma* is the place of God's presence.

God continues by promising that God will give David a house, a dynasty, rather than David building a house or a temple for God.

> When your days are fulfilled and you lie down with your ancestors, I will raise up your offspring after you, who shall come forth from your body, and I will establish his kingdom. He shall build a house for my name, and I will establish the throne of his kingdom forever. I will be a father to him, and he shall be a son to me. (2 Sam 7:12–14)

It might seem that the son promised is Solomon, the one who will build a house for God, the great temple in Jerusalem. However, Solomon's throne of his kingdom will certainly not be established forever.

Luke is particularly aware of the problem of Solomon's temple. In Stephen's long speech in Acts 7, before he dies a martyr's death, Stephen presents Solomon's building of the temple as a retrograde act that is judged badly. Again, here, the importance of 2 Samuel 7 is evident.

> Our ancestors had the tent of witness in the wilderness, as God directed when he spoke to Moses, ordering him to make it according to the pattern he had seen. Our ancestors in turn brought it in with Joshua when they dispossessed the nations that God drove out before our ancestors. And it was there until the time of David, who found favor with God and asked that he might find a dwelling place for the house of Jacob. But it was Solomon who built a house for him. Yet the Most High does not dwell in houses made with human hands; as the prophet says, "Heaven is my throne, and the earth is my footstool. What kind of house will you build for me, says the Lord, or what is the place of my rest?" (Acts 7:44–49)

David found favor with God, but Solomon built a house for him. The contrast is dramatic.

Kings build palaces so that the people can come to them. Temples are also imposing places that enshrine God's presence and the people seeking to worship God come to the temple. However, the God of David seeks to dwell in a *kataluma* so that God can move around and be among the people. It is precisely this reality that prompted the building of the Tent of Witness (or "Tent of Meeting" in Hebrew) at Sinai. God had said, "Have them make me a sanctuary, so that I may dwell among them" (Exod 25:8). In God's words, communicated by Nathan to David, God is described as "moving about." This is possible in a tent that is portable but impossible in a house that is fixed and stable. God seeks to move about among God's people.

In the Hebrew expression, the verb used for God's moving about is the same verb used in Genesis 3:8, a description of God's walking about in the Garden of Eden. "They heard the sound of the LORD God walking in the garden at the time of the evening breeze" (Gen 3:8). In the Garden, God walked/moved about in the intimacy of a relationship with Adam and Eve, a relationship profoundly wounded by the sin of eating the forbidden fruit and hiding from God. God seeks to walk/move about with them, but they have turned away from God. The construction of the Tent of Witness is an act that restores the lost intimacy; God can walk again among the people, God can be present.

In reflecting on the depths of meaning communicated by Luke's use of the word *kataluma*, where there is no room for Jesus when he is born, but which is prepared when he offers his body as food for the world, the enigma remains concerning how to translate this term. The mystery is deepened when the reader begins to realize that the *kataluma* in which God seeks to dwell, to move about among the people, is the Body of Jesus. The reader is called to ask whether now that place is ready to be the very place where Jesus can be encountered as God's presence among humanity.

Luke's second volume, the Acts of the Apostles, will document the adventure of establishing "tents of witness" in which Jesus can be encountered, tents that fill the world, stretching their curtains to accommodate all who come in. Isaiah again provides the language that prefigures the foundation of a Church that is the Body of Christ, welcoming in all peoples:

> Sing, O barren one who did not bear;
>> burst into song and shout,
>> you who have not been in labor!
> For the children of the desolate woman will be more
>> than the children of her that is married, says the LORD.
> Enlarge the site of your tent,
>> and let the curtains of your habitations be stretched out;
> do not hold back; lengthen your cords
>> and strengthen your stakes.
> For you will spread out to the right and to the left,
>> and your descendants will possess the nations
>> and will settle the desolate towns. (Isa 54:1–3)

Emmanuel, God Is with Us

In the Gospel of Matthew, the connection between Jesus and God's presence is also seminal. There is an aspect of the name of the child that is unique to Matthew and that echoes the focus on the presence of God in Jesus. Only in this book of the Gospel does Jesus have another name. This becomes clear in paying attention to the entirety of what Matthew tells the reader concerning the name of the child. "'You are to name him Jesus, for he will save his people from their sins.' All this took place to fulfil what had been spoken by the Lord through the prophet: 'Look, the virgin shall conceive and bear a son, and they shall name him Emmanuel,' which means, 'God is with us'" (Matt 1:21–23). Is the child's name Jesus or Emmanuel? Or is it both?

Joseph names him Jesus, but he will also be known as Emmanuel, "God is with us." This is a very important feature in the Gospel of Matthew. Jesus in fact has two names, both of which signify his vocation. The first name, Jesus (Yeshua), signifies that he will save his people from their sins. The second name, Emmanuel, signifies that God is with the people, an ongoing presence of God in the person of God's Son, Jesus. The name Emmanuel is hinted at again in the fourth of Jesus's five discourses in Matthew's Gospel, the discourse about the Church. There Jesus says, "For where two or three are gathered in my name, I am there among them" (18:20). *I am there among them* are words that refer directly to the ongoing presence of Jesus. However, the mystery of the second name is only fully understood at the end of the Gospel of Matthew. When Jesus, risen from the dead, encounters his disciples on the high mountain, he says to them, "Remember, I am with you always, to the end of the age" (Matt 28:20). In the original Greek, the words *God is with us* parallel the words *I am with you*. The opening of a parentheses with Emmanuel in chapter 1 is brought to a close in the words of Jesus in chapter 28. *Emmanuel*, like *Jesus*, is a name that signifies who this child is in the lives of those who receive him.

> Let us pray
> that we might be ready to receive him who comes as
>   Emmanuel.
> Might we be as tents, as tabernacles, as sanctuaries,
> carrying God's presence into the world
> that is waiting for light and life.
> Pray for us, Holy Mary, prophetic Mother of God.
> Pray for us, Saint Joseph, son of Jacob and father of Jesus!

Group Discussion

Refer to the introduction for tips on conducting a group discussion.

Questions for further reflection (select a few questions from the list below that you feel will help stimulate reflection and discussion; you could also use your own questions):

1. What strikes you as you read these two verses again side by side? Would you agree that the first description prepares for the second, while the second sheds light on the first?
   "She gave birth to her firstborn son and wrapped him in bands of cloth, and laid him in a manger, because there was no place for them in the inn." (Luke 2:7)
   "He took it down, and wrapped it in a linen cloth and laid it in a rock-hewn tomb where no one had ever been laid." (Luke 23:53)
2. Do you recognize the prophetic nature of Mary wrapping Jesus in bands of cloth and laying Jesus in a manger, a place that is meant for food? How does this develop your understanding of the infancy narratives?
3. What does the image of the manger, and its evoking of Isaiah's pain at the spiritual state of the people of God, say to you today?
4. Does anything strike you about Jesus's additional name, *Emmanuel*, "God is with us"?
5. What meaning do you derive from the gifts of gold, frankincense, and myrrh?
6. What connection do you see between Luke's use of the word *kataluma*, translated as "inn" and "guest room" respectively, when speaking about Jesus's place of birth and the Passover meal, where he instituted the Eucharist?
7. Do you ever seek to build a solid house for the God who desires to live in a tent? Do you feel that you ever seek to create God in your own image and likeness?
8. For you, where is God's *kataluma* right now, and what does it say to you about God that God wants to dwell and move about among the people?
9. What can you do in your own life to make a place for an intimate encounter with Jesus?
10. Is your church a "Tent of Witness," a true "Body of Christ," that is welcoming to all people?

Notes

Foreword

1. Regina Caeli, Sixth Sunday of Easter (May 17, 2009), https://www.vatican.va/content/benedict-xvi/en/angelus/2009/documents/hf_ben-xvi_reg_20090517.html.

2. See Bargil Pixner, *With Jesus through Galilee according to the Fifth Gospel* (Rosh Pina: Corazin Publishing, 1992), 137.

Preface

1. "Reading backwards" is the title of a book that has partially inspired these chapters. Richard B. Hays, *Reading Backwards: Figural Christology and the Fourfold Gospel Witness* (Waco, TX: Baylor University Press, 2014).

Chapter 1

1. Here and elsewhere, the citations from the Bible are from the New Revised Standard Version (NRSV), although sometimes modified so that the translation concords better with the Greek of the ancient Septuagint version and the New Testament. Modern translations of the Old Testament derive from the Hebrew original,

but the writers of the New Testament based themselves on the ancient Greek version.

Chapter 3

1. The scene of Miryam's dance is beautifully depicted in the Disney animated film *The Prince of Egypt*, and can be viewed online at www.youtube.com/watch?v=bUKVooRZhy8&t=1s.